Introduction

In an era defined by rapid technological advancement, globalization, and unprecedented social change, the principles of effective leadership have never been more critical. "The Power Playbook: Strategies for Modern Leadership" revisits and revitalizes the timeless wisdom of Niccolò Machiavelli's "The Prince," adapting its insights to the contemporary landscape of politics, business, and personal success.

Machiavelli's work, originally penned in the tumultuous political environment of Renaissance Italy, offered a candid exploration of power dynamics, strategy, and governance. Today, leaders face challenges that are equally complex but vastly different in nature. From navigating digital transformation and managing global teams to addressing ethical dilemmas and fostering innovation, the demands on modern leaders are both diverse and dynamic.

This updated guide distills Machiavelli's core tenets into actionable strategies for today's leaders. It explores the nuanced art of balancing ambition with ethics, the importance of adaptability in a rapidly changing world, and the strategic use of influence and persuasion. By blending historical insights with contemporary examples, "The Power Playbook" provides a comprehensive road-map for aspiring leaders to thrive in the 21st century.

Key Themes

Adaptive Leadership: Understanding the importance of flexibility and the ability to pivot strategies in response to evolving circumstances.

Ethical Pragmatism: Navigating the delicate balance between moral integrity and practical decision-making in leadership roles.

Digital Diplomacy: Leveraging technology and digital platforms to enhance influence, communication, and strategic outreach.

Global Perspective: Appreciating cultural diversity and leading with a global mindset in an interconnected world.

Innovation and Change Management: Cultivating an environment that encourages innovation while effectively managing change.

Chapters

Chapter 1: Introduction to Modern Leadership

Chapter 2: The Foundations of Effective Leadership

Chapter 3: Developing Emotional Intelligence

Chapter 4: Strategic Vision and Innovation

Chapter 5: Leading Diverse and Inclusive Teams

Chapter 6: Effective Communication and Influence

Chapter 7: Decision-Making and Problem-Solving

Chapter 8: Navigating Change and Transformation

Chapter 9: Building High-Performance Teams

Chapter 10: Conflict Resolution and Negotiation

Chapter 11: Fostering a Culture of Continuous Learning

Chapter 12: Leveraging Technology and Digital Transformation

Chapter 13: Ethical Decision-Making in a Globalized World

Chapter 14: The Future of Leadership

Chapter 15: Building Resilient Organizations

Chapter 16: Leading with Purpose and Vision

Chapter 17: The Role of Mentorship and Coaching in Leadership Development

CHAPTER 1: INTRODUCTION TO MODERN LEADERSHIP

Overview of leadership evolution

Leadership has evolved significantly from its early days of autocratic rule, where a single leader made decisions without input from others, to today's more dynamic and inclusive approaches. In the past, leadership was often associated with power and control, with leaders seen as the primary decision-makers who wielded authority over their followers. However, this top-down approach has gradually given way to more collaborative and participative styles of leadership.

The industrial revolution marked a significant shift in leadership styles as organizations grew larger and more complex. During this period, scientific management principles emphasized efficiency, productivity, and hierarchical structures. Leaders were expected to manage operations, enforce discipline, and maximize output.

In the latter half of the 20th century, the human relations movement emerged, highlighting the importance of employee satisfaction and motivation. Theories such as Maslow's hierarchy of needs and Herzberg's two-factor theory emphasized that employees' psychological needs must be met for optimal performance. This shift led to a greater focus on leadership styles that emphasized empathy, communication, and employee engagement.

Today, leadership is seen as a multifaceted and dynamic process that involves influencing and inspiring others to achieve common goals. Modern leadership recognizes the value of diverse perspectives, emotional intelligence, and ethical behavior. It is no longer just about directing and controlling but about empowering and enabling others to succeed.

Importance of adaptability in contemporary leadership

In today's fast-paced and constantly changing environment, adaptability is crucial for effective leadership. The rapid advancement of technology, globalization, and shifting workforce demographics have created a complex and uncertain landscape. Leaders must be able to pivot quickly in response to new challenges and opportunities, requiring a mindset that embraces change and encourages flexibility within the organization.

Adaptable leaders are those who can anticipate changes, respond to unexpected events, and adjust their strategies accordingly. They are comfortable with ambiguity and are skilled at navigating through uncertainty. This adaptability allows them to stay ahead of the competition, seize new opportunities, and lead their organizations through periods of transformation.

For instance, during the COVID-19 pandemic, many organizations had to rapidly transition to remote work. Leaders who were adaptable and open to new ways of working were able to successfully guide their teams through this transition, while those who resisted change struggled to maintain productivity and morale.

Adaptable leaders also recognize the importance of continuous learning and development. They invest in their own growth and encourage their teams to do the same. By staying informed about industry trends, technological advancements, and emerging best practices, they ensure that their organizations remain competitive and relevant in an ever-changing world.

Key Themes of the Book
This book covers essential topics for modern leaders, providing actionable insights and practical strategies to help leaders excel in their roles. The key themes explored in this book include:

The Foundations of Effective Leadership: Understanding the core qualities and principles that form the foundation of successful leadership, including integrity, accountability, and empathy.

Developing Emotional Intelligence: Exploring the components of emotional intelligence (EI) and how leaders can apply EI to enhance their effectiveness, build stronger relationships, and create positive work environments.

Strategic Vision and Innovation: Crafting a compelling vision, fostering a culture of innovation, and aligning strategy with vision to drive organizational success.

Leading Diverse and Inclusive Teams: The importance of diversity and inclusion, strategies for creating an inclusive environment, and the benefits of diverse teams.

Effective Communication and Influence: Key communication skills for leaders, techniques for persuasive communication, and building influence within and outside the organization.

Decision-Making and Problem-Solving: Decision-making frameworks, balancing data-driven and intuitive decision-making, and effective problem-solving techniques.

Navigating Change and Transformation: Leading through change, strategies for managing resistance, and case studies of successful transformations.

Building High-Performance Teams: Characteristics of high-performance teams, team-building strategies, and leading remote and hybrid teams.

Conflict Resolution and Negotiation: Techniques for resolving conflicts, negotiation strategies, and case studies of effective conflict resolution.

Fostering a Culture of Continuous Learning: The importance of lifelong learning, creating a learning culture, and encouraging professional development.

Leveraging Technology and Digital Transformation: Understanding digital transformation, embracing new technologies, developing a digital strategy, and ensuring cybersecurity.

Ethical Decision-Making in a Globalized World: Navigating global ethical challenges, promoting corporate social responsibility (CSR), addressing ethical dilemmas, and building an ethical organizational culture.

The Future of Leadership: Embracing technological advancements, leading in remote and hybrid work environments, fostering diversity and inclusion, addressing global challenges, and ensuring continuous learning and adaptability.

Building Resilient Organizations: Understanding organizational resilience, proactive risk management, fostering organizational agility, cultivating a strong organizational culture, leveraging technology for resilience, and learning from crises.

Leading with Purpose and Vision: Defining organizational purpose, crafting a compelling vision, communicating purpose and vision, aligning strategy with purpose and vision, and measuring impact and success.

The Role of Mentorship and Coaching in Leadership Development: The importance of mentorship, benefits of coaching, creating a mentorship program, implementing effective coaching, and encouraging a culture of feedback.

Each chapter delves into these themes, providing leaders with the knowledge and tools needed to navigate the complexities of modern leadership and achieve long-term success. By embracing these principles, modern leaders can enhance their effectiveness, drive innovation, and leave a lasting impact on their organizations and society.

CHAPTER 2: THE FOUNDATIONS OF EFFECTIVE LEADERSHIP

Core Leadership Qualities and Principles

Effective leadership is built on a foundation of essential qualities and principles that guide leaders in their actions and decisions. These core qualities include integrity, accountability, empathy, resilience, and visionary thinking.

Integrity: Integrity is the cornerstone of effective leadership. It involves being honest, ethical, and consistent in actions and decisions. Leaders with integrity build trust with their teams and stakeholders, creating a strong moral compass for the organization.

Example: *Warren Buffett, CEO of Berkshire Hathaway, is known for his integrity and transparent communication, which has garnered trust from investors and employees alike.*

Accountability: Accountability means taking responsibility for one's actions and the outcomes of those actions. Effective leaders hold themselves and their teams accountable, fostering a culture of ownership and reliability.

Example: *Satya Nadella, CEO of Microsoft, emphasizes accountability and learning from failures, which has helped transform Microsoft's culture and performance.*

Empathy: Empathy is the ability to understand and share the feelings of others. Empathetic leaders connect with their team members on a personal level, creating a supportive and inclusive environment.

Example: *Oprah Winfrey, media mogul and philanthropist, is renowned for her empathetic leadership style, which has made her a beloved figure and influential leader.*

Resilience: Resilience is the capacity to recover from setbacks and adapt to change. Resilient leaders remain steadfast in the face of challenges, maintaining their composure and guiding their teams through adversity.

Example: Elon Musk, CEO of Tesla and SpaceX, has demonstrated resilience by overcoming numerous obstacles and setbacks in his pursuit of innovative and ambitious goals.

Visionary Thinking: Visionary thinking involves having a clear and compelling vision for the future. Visionary leaders inspire and motivate their teams by articulating a future state that aligns with the organization's values and goals.

Example: Jeff Bezos, founder of Amazon, had a visionary approach to e-commerce, which transformed Amazon into one of the most successful companies in the world.

Building Trust and Credibility

Trust and credibility are vital for effective leadership. They are earned through consistent, ethical behavior and transparent communication. Leaders must demonstrate competence, reliability, and fairness to build and maintain trust with their teams and stakeholders.

Consistent Behavior: Consistency in actions and decisions reinforces trust. Leaders who act consistently with their values and principles are seen as reliable and trustworthy.

Example: Angela Merkel, former Chancellor of Germany, was known for her consistent and principled leadership, which earned her respect and trust both domestically and internationally.

Transparent Communication: Open and honest communication fosters trust and credibility. Leaders should communicate clearly, provide regular updates, and be open to feedback.

Example: Jacinda Ardern, Prime Minister of New Zealand, is praised for her transparent communication style, especially during crises such as the COVID-19 pandemic.

Demonstrating Competence: Leaders must be knowledgeable and skilled in their roles. Demonstrating competence builds confidence in their ability to lead effectively.

Example: Mary Barra, CEO of General Motors, has demonstrated competence in navigating the automotive industry, driving innovation and growth within the company.

Fairness and Equity: Treating all team members fairly and equitably strengthens trust and credibility. Leaders must ensure that decisions and actions are just and impartial.

Example: Tim Cook, CEO of Apple, has emphasized fairness and inclusion, fostering a culture of equity within the organization.

Ethical Leadership

Ethical leadership is about making decisions that are morally sound and in the best interests of all stakeholders. It involves upholding strong ethical standards, fostering a culture of integrity, and considering the broader impact of decisions.

Setting Ethical Standards: Leaders must establish and communicate clear ethical standards for the organization. This includes creating a code of conduct and ensuring that all employees understand and adhere to these standards.

Example: Patagonia's commitment to environmental and social responsibility is reflected in its ethical standards and business practices.

Fostering an Ethical Culture: Creating a culture of integrity involves leading by example and promoting ethical behavior at all levels of the organization. Leaders should recognize and reward ethical behavior and address unethical conduct promptly.

Example: Howard Schultz, former CEO of Starbucks, emphasized ethical sourcing and fair trade practices, embedding these values into the company's culture.

Considering Stakeholder Impact: Ethical leaders consider the impact of their decisions on all stakeholders, including employees, customers, suppliers, and the community. They strive to balance the needs and interests of different groups.

Example: Paul Polman, former CEO of Unilever, focused on sustainability and social responsibility, ensuring that the company's actions benefited a wide range of stakeholders.

Long-term Thinking: Ethical leadership involves thinking beyond short-term gains and considering the long-term consequences of decisions. Leaders should prioritize sustainable growth and the well-being of future generations.

Example: Yvon Chouinard, founder of Patagonia, has long advocated for environmentally sustainable business practices, prioritizing long-term ecological health over short-term profits.

Conclusion
The foundations of effective leadership are built on core qualities such as integrity, accountability, empathy, resilience, and visionary thinking. Building trust and credibility through consistent behavior, transparent communication, demonstrating competence, and ensuring fairness is crucial. Ethical leadership, which involves setting and upholding ethical standards, fostering an ethical culture, considering stakeholder impact, and prioritizing long-term thinking, is essential for sustainable success.

By understanding and embracing these foundational principles, leaders can navigate the complexities of modern leadership and create positive, lasting impacts on their organizations and society. The subsequent chapters will delve deeper into specific aspects of leadership, providing practical insights and strategies to help leaders enhance their effectiveness and drive organizational success.

CHAPTER 3: DEVELOPING EMOTIONAL INTELLIGENCE

Understanding Emotional Intelligence (EI)

Emotional Intelligence (EI) is the ability to recognize, understand, manage, and effectively use emotions in ourselves and others. It is a critical component of effective leadership, as it influences how leaders manage behavior, navigate social complexities, and make personal decisions that achieve positive results. Daniel Goleman, a leading psychologist, popularized the concept of EI and identified five key components: self-awareness, self-regulation, motivation, empathy, and social skills.

Components of EI: Self-awareness, Self-regulation, Motivation, Empathy, Social Skills

Self-awareness

Self-awareness is the foundation of emotional intelligence. It involves recognizing one's own emotions, strengths, weaknesses, values, and drivers and understanding their impact on others. Leaders with high self-awareness are often more reflective and open to feedback.

Example: *A leader who is aware of their stress triggers can proactively manage their reactions, ensuring they remain calm and composed during high-pressure situations.*

Practical Tips:

Keep a journal to track your emotions and reactions to different situations.

Seek feedback from trusted colleagues to gain insights into your behavior and its impact on others.

Self-regulation

Self-regulation refers to the ability to control or redirect disruptive emotions and impulses and adapt to changing circumstances. Leaders who can manage their emotions effectively are better equipped to handle stress and maintain a positive outlook.

Example: *A leader who practices self-regulation might take a few deep breaths before responding to a challenging email, ensuring their response is measured and constructive.*

Practical Tips:
Practice mindfulness and meditation to enhance your ability to regulate emotions.

Develop a routine for dealing with stress, such as regular exercise or relaxation techniques.

Motivation
Motivation in the context of EI is characterized by a passion for work that goes beyond money or status, driven by an internal desire to achieve goals and personal growth. Motivated leaders are optimistic, committed, and persistent even in the face of setbacks.

Example: *A leader motivated by a sense of purpose might stay focused and enthusiastic about a project despite encountering significant obstacles.*

Practical Tips:
Set personal and professional goals that align with your values and passions.

Celebrate small achievements to maintain motivation and momentum.

Empathy
Empathy is the ability to understand and share the feelings of others. It involves recognizing others' emotional states, being sensitive to their needs, and valuing diverse perspectives. Empathetic leaders build strong relationships and create inclusive environments.

Example: *A leader who practices empathy might recognize when a team member is struggling and offer support or adjust their workload.*

Practical Tips:
Actively listen to others without interrupting or judging. Put yourself in others' shoes to better understand their perspectives and emotions.

Social Skills
Social skills involve managing relationships to move people in desired directions. Leaders with strong social skills are adept at conflict resolution, building networks, and fostering teamwork. They are effective communicators and influencers.

Example: *A leader with strong social skills might successfully mediate a conflict between team members, ensuring a positive and collaborative outcome.*

Practical Tips:
Work on your communication skills, including active listening, clear articulation, and non-verbal cues. Invest time in building and maintaining professional relationships.

Applying EI in Leadership
Emotional intelligence is not just a theoretical concept; it has practical applications that can significantly enhance leadership effectiveness. Here's how leaders can apply EI in various aspects of their roles:

Building Stronger Teams
Leaders with high EI are adept at understanding the dynamics of their teams and fostering a positive, collaborative environment. They recognize individual strengths and weaknesses and can tailor their approach to meet the needs of each team member.

Example: *An emotionally intelligent leader might notice that a team member is feeling overwhelmed and offer support or delegate tasks to balance the workload.*

Enhancing Communication
Effective communication is a hallmark of emotionally intelligent leaders. They listen actively, convey their messages clearly, and are attuned to the emotional undertones of conversations.

Example: *During a team meeting, an emotionally intelligent leader might notice non-verbal cues indicating confusion and take the time to clarify their points.*

Improving Conflict Resolution

Conflict is inevitable in any organization, but leaders with high EI can navigate conflicts with empathy and tact. They approach disagreements with a solution-oriented mindset and strive to understand all perspectives involved.

Example: *An emotionally intelligent leader might facilitate a discussion between conflicting parties, helping them find common ground and resolve their differences.*

Fostering a Positive Work Environment

Leaders with high EI create environments where employees feel valued, respected, and motivated. They are approachable, supportive, and attentive to the well-being of their team members.

Example: *An emotionally intelligent leader might implement regular check-ins with team members to gauge their satisfaction and address any concerns.*

Driving Change and Innovation

Change can be challenging, but leaders with high EI are skilled at managing the emotional aspects of change. They communicate the vision and benefits of change effectively and support their teams through transitions.

Example: *During a major organizational change, an emotionally intelligent leader might hold open forums for employees to express their concerns and provide reassurance and clarity.*

Developing Your Emotional Intelligence

Developing emotional intelligence is an ongoing process that requires self-reflection, practice, and a commitment to personal growth. Here are some strategies to help you enhance your EI:

Self-assessment: Regularly evaluate your emotional strengths and areas for improvement. Tools such as personality assessments and feedback from others can provide valuable insights.

Mindfulness Practices: Engage in mindfulness activities such as meditation, deep breathing exercises, or yoga. These practices can help you become more aware of your emotions and improve your ability to regulate them.

Seek Feedback: Encourage honest feedback from colleagues, mentors, and team members. Use this feedback to identify blind spots and areas for development.

Emotional Journaling: Keep a journal to track your emotional responses to various situations. Reflect on what triggered these emotions and how you managed them.

Empathy Exercises: Practice empathy by actively listening to others and trying to understand their perspectives. Engage in conversations that challenge you to see things from different viewpoints.

Professional Development: Invest in training and development programs focused on emotional intelligence. Workshops, seminars, and coaching sessions can provide valuable skills and techniques.

Build Relationships: Strengthen your social skills by building and nurturing professional relationships. Attend networking events, participate in team activities, and seek opportunities to collaborate with others.

Manage Stress: Develop healthy coping mechanisms for stress, such as regular exercise, hobbies, or spending time with loved ones. Managing stress effectively is crucial for maintaining emotional balance.

Conclusion
Emotional intelligence is a vital component of effective leadership, influencing how leaders interact with their teams, make decisions, and navigate the complexities of the modern workplace. By understanding and developing the five key components of EI—self-awareness, self-regulation, motivation, empathy, and social skills—leaders can enhance their ability to connect with others, manage stress, and drive positive outcomes.

Incorporating emotional intelligence into your leadership style not only improves your personal effectiveness but also creates a more supportive, collaborative, and productive work environment. As you continue to develop your EI, you will be better equipped to lead with empathy, resilience, and vision, inspiring your team to achieve their full potential and driving your organization toward success.

CHAPTER 4: STRATEGIC VISION AND INNOVATION

Crafting a Compelling Vision

A compelling vision is a clear, inspirational, and achievable picture of the future that guides an organization's strategic direction. It aligns and motivates stakeholders, setting a framework for decision-making and prioritizing efforts.

Defining the Vision: A vision statement should articulate the organization's long-term goals and the impact it aims to have. It should be ambitious yet attainable, reflecting the core values and mission of the organization.

Example: Tesla's vision statement is "to create the most compelling car company of the 21st century by driving the world's transition to electric vehicles."

Involving Stakeholders: Engaging key stakeholders in the vision-creation process ensures buy-in and alignment. This can include employees, customers, partners, and investors.

Example: A tech company might hold workshops and brainstorming sessions with employees to gather diverse perspectives and ideas for the vision statement.

Communicating the Vision: Clearly communicating the vision is crucial for its success. Leaders should consistently reinforce the vision through various channels, such as meetings, newsletters, and company events.

Example: Steve Jobs was known for his ability to articulate Apple's vision during product launches and public addresses, inspiring both employees and customers.

Aligning Strategies with Vision: All strategic initiatives should align with the vision to ensure coherence and focus. This involves setting goals, objectives, and key performance indicators (KPIs) that support the vision.

Example: *A health-care organization's vision to "improve patient outcomes through innovative technology" might align its strategies towards investing in advanced medical equipment and training programs.*

Fostering a Culture of Innovation
Innovation is the lifeblood of any forward-thinking organization. It involves creating a culture that encourages creativity, experimentation, and continuous improvement.

Encouraging Creativity: Leaders should create an environment where employees feel safe to express ideas and take risks without fear of failure. This can be achieved through open forums, idea incubators, and innovation labs.

Example: *Google's 20% time policy allows employees to spend 20% of their work hours on projects they are passionate about, fostering innovation.*

Providing Resources and Support: Innovation requires resources such as time, funding, and access to technology. Leaders should ensure that teams have the necessary support to explore and develop new ideas.

Example: *3M allocates a portion of its budget to fund employee-driven innovation projects, leading to products like Post-it Notes and Scotch Tape.*

Recognizing and Rewarding Innovation: Recognizing and rewarding innovative efforts encourages a continuous flow of ideas. This can include monetary rewards, public recognition, or career advancement opportunities.

Example: *Adobe's Kick-box program provides employees with a toolkit and funding to develop and test new ideas, with successful projects being publicly celebrated.*

Embracing Failure as a Learning Opportunity: An innovative culture views failure as a stepping stone to success. Leaders should encourage teams to learn from their mistakes and iterate on their ideas.

Example: *Amazon's willingness to experiment and accept failures, like the Fire Phone, has led to successful innovations such as AWS and Kindle.*

Driving Strategic Innovation
Strategic innovation involves integrating innovation into the organization's strategic plan, ensuring that it contributes to long-term goals and competitive advantage.

Identifying Opportunities for Innovation: Leaders should continuously scan the environment for opportunities to innovate, such as emerging technologies, market trends, and customer needs.

Example: *Netflix identified the opportunity to transition from DVD rentals to streaming services, revolutionizing the entertainment industry.*

Developing an Innovation Strategy: An innovation strategy outlines the organization's approach to fostering and managing innovation. It should include goals, priorities, and metrics for measuring success.

Example: *Apple's innovation strategy focuses on creating a seamless ecosystem of hardware, software, and services that enhance user experience.*

Integrating Innovation into the Business Model: Innovation should be embedded into the business model, influencing how the organization creates, delivers, and captures value.

Example: *Uber's business model innovation disrupted traditional taxi services by leveraging mobile technology and a gig economy workforce.*

Collaborating for Innovation: Partnerships and collaborations can enhance innovation efforts by bringing in diverse perspectives and expertise. This can include alliances with other companies, academic institutions, and research organizations.

Example: *Pharmaceutical companies often collaborate with academic researchers to develop new drugs and therapies.*

Overcoming Barriers to Innovation
Despite its importance, innovation often faces several barriers that leaders must navigate and overcome.

Cultural Resistance: Organizational culture can resist change, particularly if it is risk-averse or hierarchical. Leaders must work to shift the culture towards one that embraces innovation.

Example: A traditional manufacturing company might implement training programs and workshops to foster an innovative mindset among employees.

Resource Constraints: Limited resources can hinder innovation efforts. Leaders should prioritize innovation projects and allocate resources strategically.

Example: A start-up with limited funding might focus on high-impact, low-cost innovations and seek external investment to scale successful projects.

Structural Barriers: Organizational structures that are too rigid can stifle innovation. Leaders should consider adopting more flexible and agile structures.

Example: Implementing cross-functional teams can break down silos and promote collaborative innovation.

Leadership Challenges: Leadership can be a barrier if leaders are not supportive of innovation. Leaders must champion innovation, provide clear direction, and empower employees to innovate.

Example: A CEO who regularly communicates the importance of innovation and provides the necessary support can significantly boost the organization's innovation efforts.

Case Studies of Successful Innovation

Tesla: Tesla's innovation in electric vehicles and renewable energy solutions has revolutionized the automotive and energy industries. Its commitment to a clear vision and continuous innovation has driven its success.

Key Takeaway: Aligning innovation with a compelling vision and investing in R&D can lead to industry disruption and long-term success.

Airbnb: Airbnb's platform innovation transformed the hospitality industry by creating a marketplace for unique, short-term accommodations. Its success is rooted in a user-centric approach and leveraging technology.

Key Takeaway: Understanding market needs and leveraging digital platforms can create new business models and drive growth.

Spotify: Spotify's innovation in music streaming services disrupted the music industry by offering a vast library of music through a subscription model. Its use of data analytics and personalized recommendations has enhanced user experience.

Key Takeaway: Using data and technology to personalize services can significantly enhance customer satisfaction and loyalty.

Conclusion

Strategic vision and innovation are integral to effective leadership and organizational success. By crafting a compelling vision, fostering a culture of innovation, driving strategic innovation, and overcoming barriers, leaders can position their organizations at the forefront of their industries.

Embracing these principles not only ensures sustainable growth but also inspires and motivates teams to achieve extraordinary results. As leaders continue to navigate the complexities of the modern business landscape, the ability to think strategically and innovate will remain a crucial determinant of success.

CHAPTER 5: LEADING DIVERSE AND INCLUSIVE TEAMS

The Importance of Diversity and Inclusion

In today's globalized world, diversity and inclusion (D&I) are not just moral imperatives but strategic advantages. Diverse teams bring a variety of perspectives, leading to more innovative solutions and better decision-making. Inclusive environments ensure that every team member feels valued and empowered to contribute their best.

Enhanced Innovation and Creativity: Diverse teams leverage a range of experiences and viewpoints, leading to more creative problem-solving and innovation.

Example: A tech company with a culturally diverse team might develop products that appeal to a broader, global audience, as they consider varied user needs and preferences.

Improved Decision-Making: Inclusive teams are better at considering different angles of a problem, leading to more balanced and effective decisions.

Example: A diverse board of directors can provide a wider range of insights and expertise, improving governance and strategic direction.

Attracting and Retaining Talent: Companies committed to D&I are more attractive to top talent, particularly in a competitive job market where employees value inclusive cultures.

Example: A company known for its inclusive practices may attract highly skilled candidates who seek a supportive and equitable work environment.

Reflecting the Market and Community: Organizations that mirror the diversity of their markets and communities are better positioned to understand and serve their customers.

Example: A consumer goods company with a diverse marketing team can create campaigns that resonate with different demographic groups.

The Importance of Diversity and Inclusion

In today's globalized world, diversity and inclusion (D&I) are not just moral imperatives but strategic advantages. Diverse teams bring a variety of perspectives, leading to more innovative solutions and better decision-making. Inclusive environments ensure that every team member feels valued and empowered to contribute their best.

Enhanced Innovation and Creativity: Diverse teams leverage a range of experiences and viewpoints, leading to more creative problem-solving and innovation.

Example: A tech company with a culturally diverse team might develop products that appeal to a broader, global audience, as they consider varied user needs and preferences.

Improved Decision-Making: Inclusive teams are better at considering different angles of a problem, leading to more balanced and effective decisions.

Example: A diverse board of directors can provide a wider range of insights and expertise, improving governance and strategic direction.

Attracting and Retaining Talent: Companies committed to D&I are more attractive to top talent, particularly in a competitive job market where employees value inclusive cultures.

Example: A company known for its inclusive practices may attract highly skilled candidates who seek a supportive and equitable work environment.

Reflecting the Market and Community: Organizations that mirror the diversity of their markets and communities are better positioned to understand and serve their customers.

Example: A consumer goods company with a diverse marketing team can create campaigns that resonate with different demographic groups.

Building a Diverse Team
Building a diverse team involves intentional recruitment, hiring, and development practices that promote equity and inclusion.

Diverse Recruitment Strategies: Proactively seek candidates from various backgrounds through partnerships with diverse professional organizations, attending job fairs, and using inclusive language in job postings.

Example: *A tech firm might partner with coding boot camps that focus on training women and minorities in software development.*

Bias-Free Hiring Practices: Implement structured interviews and diverse hiring panels to minimize unconscious bias and ensure a fair hiring process.

Example: *Using standardized interview questions and evaluation criteria can help reduce bias and ensure candidates are assessed equitably.*

Inclusive On-boarding: Create on-boarding programs that emphasize the organization's commitment to D&I and provide new hires with the resources and support they need to succeed.

Example: *Providing mentorship programs and diversity training during on-boarding can help new employees feel welcomed and included from day one.*

Continuous Development and Promotion: Offer ongoing training, mentorship, and leadership development programs to ensure all employees have opportunities for growth and advancement.

Example: *A company might offer leadership training programs specifically designed for underrepresented groups to help them advance within the organization.*

Creating an Inclusive Culture
An inclusive culture is one where all employees feel respected, valued, and able to contribute fully. This involves leadership commitment, policies, and practices that support inclusivity.

Leadership Commitment: Leaders must champion D&I, setting the tone for the organization and holding themselves and others accountable for progress.

Example: A CEO who publicly commits to D&I goals and regularly reports on progress demonstrates the importance of these values to the organization.

Policies and Practices: Implement policies that promote equity, such as flexible work arrangements, parental leave, and anti-discrimination policies.

Example: A company might offer flexible working hours and remote work options to accommodate employees with diverse needs and lifestyles.

Training and Education: Provide regular training on unconscious bias, cultural competency, and inclusive leadership to raise awareness and equip employees with the skills to support D&I.

Example: Regular workshops on unconscious bias can help employees recognize and mitigate their own biases, fostering a more inclusive environment.

Employee Resource Groups (ERGs): Support ERGs that provide a platform for underrepresented groups to connect, share experiences, and influence company policies.

Example: An LGBTQ+ ERG can offer a supportive community and advocate for inclusive policies, such as gender-neutral restrooms and health-care benefits.

Measuring and Sustaining D&I Efforts
Measuring the effectiveness of D&I initiatives and ensuring their sustainability is crucial for long-term success.

Setting Goals and Metrics: Establish clear, measurable goals for D&I and track progress regularly. Metrics might include representation, employee satisfaction, and retention rates.

Example: A company might set a goal to increase the representation of women in leadership positions by a certain percentage over the next five years.

Regular Assessments: Conduct regular assessments, such as employee surveys and diversity audits, to identify areas for improvement and adjust strategies accordingly.

Example: An annual diversity audit can help identify gaps in representation and areas where inclusion efforts need to be strengthened.

Transparent Reporting: Share progress on D&I goals with employees and stakeholders to maintain transparency and accountability.

Example: Publishing an annual D&I report that outlines initiatives, progress, and areas for improvement demonstrates a commitment to continuous improvement.

Sustaining Momentum: Ensure that D&I remains a priority by embedding it into the organization's core values and strategic plans.

Example: Including D&I metrics in executive performance evaluations can help sustain focus and accountability at the highest levels of leadership.

Case Studies in Leading Diverse and Inclusive Teams

Microsoft: Microsoft has made significant strides in promoting D&I through initiatives like unconscious bias training, diverse hiring practices, and inclusive design. Their commitment is reflected in their annual D&I report, which tracks progress and outlines future goals.

Key Takeaway: Continuous commitment to D&I, backed by transparent reporting and leadership accountability, drives meaningful progress.

Sales-force: Sales-force actively promotes equality through its four pillars: equal pay, equal opportunity, equal education, and equal rights. The company conducts regular pay audits to ensure pay equity and offers extensive training and development programs.

Key Takeaway: A comprehensive approach to equality, addressing multiple aspects of D&I, creates a more equitable and inclusive workplace.

Accenture: Accenture's D&I strategy includes a strong focus on gender equality, with a goal to achieve a gender-balanced workforce by 2025. They support this with initiatives like parental leave, mentorship programs, and flexible working arrangements.

Key Takeaway: *Setting ambitious, measurable goals and providing targeted support can accelerate progress towards D&I objectives.*

Conclusion
Leading diverse and inclusive teams is essential for modern leadership. By understanding the importance of D&I, building diverse teams, creating an inclusive culture, and measuring and sustaining efforts, leaders can harness the full potential of their workforce.

Incorporating D&I into the core of leadership practices not only drives innovation and improves decision-making but also fosters a workplace where all employees feel valued and empowered. As the business landscape continues to evolve, the ability to lead diverse and inclusive teams will remain a crucial determinant of success and sustainability.

CHAPTER 6: EFFECTIVE COMMUNICATION AND INFLUENCE

The Power of Communication

Effective communication is the cornerstone of successful leadership. It enables leaders to convey their vision, motivate their teams, resolve conflicts, and build strong relationships. Mastering the art of communication involves both verbal and non-verbal skills and understanding the nuances of different communication styles.

Clarity and Conciseness: Clear and concise communication ensures that messages are understood and reduces the risk of misinterpretation. This is particularly important in conveying complex information or instructions.

Example: *A project manager who clearly outlines the goals, deadlines, and responsibilities for a project helps the team understand expectations and stay focused.*

Active Listening: Active listening involves fully engaging with the speaker, understanding their message, and responding thoughtfully. It builds trust and demonstrates respect.

Example: *During a team meeting, a leader who listens attentively to each member's input and asks clarifying questions shows that they value their team's perspectives.*

Non-Verbal Communication: Non-verbal cues, such as body language, facial expressions, and eye contact, play a significant role in how messages are perceived. Effective leaders are aware of their non-verbal communication and use it to reinforce their verbal messages.

Example: *Maintaining eye contact and nodding during a conversation can show attentiveness and agreement, strengthening the verbal message.*

Adapting Communication Styles: Different situations and audiences may require different communication styles. Effective leaders are adaptable and can modify their approach to suit the context and audience.

Example: A leader might use a more formal and structured communication style when addressing senior executives, but a more informal and engaging style during team-building activities.

Techniques for Persuasion and Influence

Influence is the ability to shape outcomes and inspire others to take action. Persuasion is a key component of influence, involving techniques that can convince others to embrace ideas, make decisions, or change behaviors.

Building Credibility: Credibility is earned through expertise, trustworthiness, and reliability. When leaders are seen as credible, their influence is significantly enhanced.

Example: A leader who consistently delivers on promises and demonstrates expertise in their field is more likely to gain the trust and support of their team.

Using Logic and Reasoning: Presenting well-reasoned arguments supported by data and evidence can persuade others by appealing to their rational side.

Example: A leader advocating for a new strategy might present data showing its potential benefits, including market research, financial projections, and case studies.

Appealing to Emotions: Emotions play a crucial role in decision-making. Persuasive leaders connect with their audience on an emotional level, using stories, analogies, and passionate delivery to evoke the desired response.

Example: A leader who shares a personal story about overcoming challenges can inspire and motivate their team to persevere through difficulties.

Social Proof and Consensus: People tend to follow the actions and beliefs of others, especially those they respect. Highlighting support from respected individuals or groups can strengthen an argument.

Example: A leader might reference the success of a similar initiative in a respected company to build support for a new project within their organization.

Reciprocity and Commitment: The principle of reciprocity involves giving something of value to encourage a return favor, while commitment involves gaining a small initial agreement that leads to larger commitments.

Example: A leader who offers assistance or resources to a colleague may find that the colleague is more willing to support their initiatives in the future.

Communicating Vision and Strategy

Effective communication of vision and strategy is essential for aligning the organization and driving collective action towards common goals.

Articulating the Vision: A compelling vision is clear, inspiring, and relatable. Leaders should communicate the vision in a way that resonates with the audience and highlights its significance.

Example: A leader might use vivid imagery and metaphors to paint a picture of the organization's future, making the vision more tangible and engaging.

Linking Strategy to Vision: It's important to clearly explain how the strategy supports the vision and how each team member's role contributes to achieving it. This creates a sense of purpose and direction.

Example: During a strategy roll-out, a leader might outline specific initiatives, explain their alignment with the vision, and show how each department's efforts contribute to the overall success.

Regular Updates and Transparency: Keeping the team informed about progress, challenges, and changes in strategy fosters transparency and trust. Regular updates help maintain alignment and motivation.

Example: A leader might hold quarterly town hall meetings to provide updates on strategic initiatives, celebrate successes, and address any concerns.

Encouraging Feedback and Dialogue: Open communication channels where team members can provide feedback and ask questions enhance understanding and engagement.

Example: A leader might implement an open-door policy or use digital platforms to encourage ongoing dialogue and feedback about the vision and strategy.

Navigating Difficult Conversations
Difficult conversations are inevitable in leadership. Whether it's providing constructive feedback, addressing conflicts, or delivering bad news, handling these conversations with skill and sensitivity is crucial.

Preparing for the Conversation: Preparation involves understanding the issue, gathering relevant information, and considering the perspective of the other party. This helps in framing the conversation constructively.

Example: Before discussing performance issues with an employee, a leader might review their performance data, consider potential reasons for under-performance, and prepare constructive feedback.

Creating a Safe Environment: Ensuring the conversation takes place in a private, respectful setting helps the other party feel safe and more open to dialogue.

Example: A leader might choose a quiet, private office for a sensitive conversation about an employee's behavior, ensuring confidentiality and respect.

Using "I" Statements and Empathy: Framing feedback using "I" statements focuses on the leader's perspective and feelings rather than placing blame. Showing empathy helps build understanding and rapport.

Example: Instead of saying, "You are always late," a leader might say, "I've noticed that you've been arriving late recently, and I'm concerned about how it's affecting the team."

Active Listening and Validation: Actively listening to the other party's perspective and validating their feelings can de-escalate tensions and foster a constructive dialogue.

Example: During a conflict resolution, a leader might listen attentively to both parties, acknowledge their feelings, and summarize their points to ensure understanding.

Finding Solutions and Agreeing on Actions: The goal of difficult conversations should be to find mutually acceptable solutions and agree on specific actions to move forward.

Example: After discussing performance issues, a leader and employee might agree on a development plan with clear goals, support mechanisms, and follow-up dates.

Building Trust Through Communication
Trust is the foundation of effective leadership and is built through consistent, honest, and transparent communication.

Consistency and Reliability: Consistently delivering on promises and communicating reliably builds trust over time. Leaders should ensure their actions align with their words.

Example: A leader who consistently meets deadlines and keeps their team informed about changes builds a reputation for reliability.

Honesty and Transparency: Being honest and transparent, even when the news is not positive, fosters trust and respect. It shows that the leader values integrity and accountability.

Example: *During organizational changes, a leader who communicates openly about challenges and uncertainties earns the trust of their team.*

Empathy and Understanding: Demonstrating empathy and understanding in communication shows that the leader cares about their team's well-being and perspectives.

Example: *A leader who takes the time to understand an employee's personal challenges and offers support demonstrates empathy and builds trust.*

Recognition and Appreciation: Regularly recognizing and appreciating team members' contributions fosters a positive and trusting work environment.

Example: *A leader who publicly acknowledges the efforts and achievements of their team members during meetings or through written communications builds a culture of appreciation and trust.*

Conclusion
Effective communication and influence are vital skills for modern leaders. By mastering clarity, active listening, and adaptability, leaders can convey their vision, motivate their teams, and build strong relationships. Techniques for persuasion and influence, coupled with transparent and empathetic communication, enhance a leader's ability to inspire and guide their organization.

Navigating difficult conversations with preparation, empathy, and active listening ensures constructive outcomes, while building trust through consistent, honest, and appreciative communication fosters a supportive and cohesive team environment. As leaders continue to develop these skills, they will be better equipped to lead with confidence, influence, and integrity, driving their organizations toward success.

CHAPTER 7: DECISION-MAKING AND PROBLEM-SOLVING

The Essentials of Effective Decision-Making
Effective decision-making is a critical component of successful leadership. It involves choosing the best course of action from various alternatives to achieve desired outcomes. The process requires a blend of analytical thinking, intuition, and the ability to manage uncertainty.

Identifying the Problem: Clearly defining the problem is the first step in effective decision-making. It involves understanding the root cause and the scope of the issue.

Example: A retail company experiencing a decline in sales might identify the problem as a mismatch between product offerings and customer preferences.

Gathering Information: Collecting relevant data and information is crucial for informed decision-making. This includes both quantitative data (such as financial metrics) and qualitative insights (such as customer feedback).

Example: A marketing team might conduct market research and analyze sales data to understand customer buying behavior and preferences.

Generating Alternatives: Brainstorming and generating multiple solutions or alternatives helps in exploring different approaches to solving the problem.

Example: A software company facing declining user engagement might consider options like improving user interface design, adding new features, or enhancing customer support.

Evaluating Alternatives: Assessing the pros and cons of each alternative, considering factors such as feasibility, cost, and potential impact, is essential for making the best choice.

Example: A business might use a decision matrix to evaluate the potential outcomes of expanding to new markets versus investing in product development.

Making the Decision: After thorough evaluation, the next step is to select the best alternative and make the decision. This should be done with confidence and a readiness to act.

Example: A company might decide to launch a new product line after assessing market demand, production capabilities, and financial projections.

Implementing the Decision: Effective implementation involves planning, resource allocation, and communicating the decision to relevant stakeholders.

Example: An organization that decides to adopt new technology might develop an implementation plan, allocate budget, and train employees on the new system.

Monitoring and Reviewing: Continuously monitoring the outcomes and reviewing the decision helps in identifying any issues and making necessary adjustments.

Example: A project manager might track the progress of a project through regular status updates and performance metrics to ensure it stays on track.

Problem-Solving Techniques
Problem-solving is closely related to decision-making and involves identifying solutions to specific issues. Effective problem-solving requires creativity, analytical skills, and a structured approach.

Root Cause Analysis: Identifying the underlying cause of a problem rather than just addressing its symptoms is crucial for effective problem-solving.

Example: *Using the "5 Whys" technique, a manufacturing company might determine that frequent machine breakdowns are due to inadequate maintenance schedules.*

Brainstorming: Encouraging open and creative thinking to generate a wide range of potential solutions.

Example: *A product development team might hold brainstorming sessions to come up with innovative features for a new product.*

SWOT Analysis: Analyzing the strengths, weaknesses, opportunities, and threats related to a problem helps in understanding the internal and external factors influencing the situation.

Example: *A start-up might conduct a SWOT analysis to identify its strengths in innovation, weaknesses in market reach, opportunities in emerging markets, and threats from established competitors.*

Cost-Benefit Analysis: Comparing the costs and benefits of different solutions to determine the most economically viable option.

Example: *An organization considering a new software system might perform a cost-benefit analysis to evaluate the financial impact and potential efficiency gains.*

Scenario Planning: Developing different scenarios based on potential future events to anticipate and plan for various outcomes.

Example: *A company might create scenarios for different economic conditions to prepare strategic responses for growth, recession, or stability.*

Pareto Analysis: Using the 80/20 rule to focus on the most significant factors contributing to a problem.

Example: *A customer service department might find that 80% of complaints are due to 20% of recurring issues, allowing them to prioritize and address these key problems.*

Decision Trees: Using a visual representation of different decision paths and their potential outcomes to systematically evaluate options.

Example: *A health-care provider might use a decision tree to determine the best treatment plan based on patient diagnosis and potential complications.*

Overcoming Decision-Making Biases
Cognitive biases can impair decision-making by leading to flawed judgments and choices. Recognizing and mitigating these biases is essential for making sound decisions.

Confirmation Bias: The tendency to seek out information that confirms pre-existing beliefs while ignoring contradictory evidence.

Mitigation: *Actively seek out and consider opposing viewpoints and evidence before making a decision.*

Anchoring Bias: Relying too heavily on the first piece of information encountered (the "anchor") when making decisions.

Mitigation: *Consider a range of information and perspectives to avoid being unduly influenced by initial data points.*

Overconfidence Bias: Overestimating one's knowledge or abilities, leading to overly optimistic decisions.

Mitigation: *Encourage critical feedback and consider worst-case scenarios to temper overconfidence.*

Availability Heuristic: Basing decisions on readily available information rather than more relevant but less accessible data.

Mitigation: Seek out comprehensive and relevant data, rather than relying on recent or memorable events.

Group-think: The tendency for group members to conform to consensus opinions without critically evaluating alternatives.

Mitigation: Foster an open and diverse team culture where dissenting opinions are valued and considered.

Sunk Cost Fallacy: Continuing a course of action due to previously invested resources, even when it is no longer viable.

Mitigation: Focus on future costs and benefits rather than past investments when making decisions.

Hindsight Bias: The tendency to see events as more predictable after they have occurred.

Mitigation: Recognize the unpredictability of events and avoid oversimplifying past decisions.

Collaborative Decision-Making

Collaborative decision-making involves engaging multiple stakeholders in the decision process, leveraging their collective expertise and perspectives.

Inclusive Participation: Involve diverse team members in the decision-making process to gather a wide range of insights and ideas.

Example: A cross-functional team might be formed to evaluate a new product launch, bringing together marketing, engineering, and sales perspectives.

Facilitating Open Dialogue: Encourage open and honest discussions where all participants feel comfortable sharing their views.

Example: Using structured meeting formats, such as round-table discussions, can ensure that all voices are heard.

Consensus Building: Strive for consensus where possible, ensuring that the decision is supported by the majority and that dissenting views are acknowledged and addressed.

Example: A nonprofit organization might use consensus-building techniques to decide on new community initiatives, ensuring broad support from stakeholders.

Decision-Making Tools: Utilize tools such as voting systems, decision matrices, and collaborative software to streamline the decision-making process and enhance transparency.

Example: An organization might use a digital collaboration platform to facilitate decision-making, allowing team members to vote and comment on proposed solutions.

Conflict Resolution: Address conflicts constructively and seek solutions that accommodate different viewpoints and interests.

Example: A mediator might be brought in to facilitate discussions and resolve conflicts within a project team, ensuring a unified decision.

Case Studies in Decision-Making and Problem-Solving

Toyota's Lean Manufacturing: Toyota's adoption of lean manufacturing principles revolutionized the automotive industry by focusing on continuous improvement and problem-solving at all levels of the organization.

Key Takeaway: Systematic problem-solving and empowering employees to identify and address issues can lead to significant operational efficiencies and innovation.

IBM's Transformation: Faced with declining profits in the 1990s, IBM made a strategic decision to shift from hardware to services and software, revitalizing the company and positioning it as a leader in technology consulting and cloud computing.

Key Takeaway: Bold, strategic decision-making, supported by thorough analysis and a willingness to adapt, can drive successful business transformation.

NASA's Apollo 13 Crisis Management: During the Apollo 13 mission, NASA's quick and effective problem-solving ensured the safe return of the astronauts after a critical system failure. The team used systematic troubleshooting and collaborative decision-making under extreme pressure.

Key Takeaway: Effective problem-solving and decision-making, especially in crisis situations, rely on clear communication, teamwork, and systematic approaches.

Conclusion
Decision-making and problem-solving are fundamental skills for modern leaders. By adopting a structured approach, leveraging diverse perspectives, and mitigating biases, leaders can make informed and effective decisions. Collaborative decision-making enhances buy-in and the quality of outcomes, while continuous learning and adaptation ensure sustained success.

Leaders who excel in decision-making and problem-solving are better equipped to navigate complexities, drive innovation, and lead their organizations to achieve their strategic goals. As the business environment continues to evolve, these skills will remain essential for effective leadership and organizational resilience.

CHAPTER 8: NAVIGATING CHANGE AND TRANSFORMATION

Understanding the Dynamics of Change
Change is a constant in today's fast-paced world, and the ability to navigate it effectively is crucial for leaders. Understanding the dynamics of change involves recognizing the various factors that drive it and the impact it has on individuals and organizations.

Drivers of Change: Change can be driven by external factors such as technological advancements, market shifts, regulatory changes, and societal trends, as well as internal factors like organizational restructuring, leadership changes, and new strategic initiatives.

Example: *A company might undergo a major transformation to adopt artificial intelligence and automation in response to technological advancements and competitive pressure.*

Impact on Individuals and Organizations: Change can evoke a range of emotions, from excitement and anticipation to fear and resistance. Understanding these reactions is key to managing the human side of change.

Example: *Employees might feel anxious about job security during a restructuring process, highlighting the need for clear communication and support from leadership.*

The Change Curve: The change curve, often based on the Kübler-Ross model, illustrates the stages individuals go through when experiencing change: shock, denial, frustration, depression, experimentation, decision, and integration.

Example: *During the implementation of a new software system, employees might initially resist the change (denial and frustration) but gradually adapt and embrace the new tool (experimentation and integration).*

Leading Change: Key Principles
Leading change effectively requires a strategic approach that encompasses clear vision, communication, stakeholder engagement, and adaptability.

Creating a Clear Vision: A compelling vision provides direction and purpose, helping stakeholders understand the reasons for change and the desired outcomes.

Example: *A health-care organization might articulate a vision for digital transformation that improves patient care, enhances efficiency, and reduces costs.*

Communicating Effectively: Transparent and frequent communication is essential for addressing concerns, providing updates, and maintaining momentum throughout the change process.

Example: *A CEO might hold regular town hall meetings and send out newsletters to keep employees informed and engaged during a major merger.*

Engaging Stakeholders: Involving key stakeholders in the planning and implementation phases fosters buy-in and collaboration. This includes identifying change champions who can advocate for and support the change.

Example: *A school district undergoing curriculum reform might involve teachers, parents, and students in the decision-making process to ensure their perspectives are considered.*

Managing Resistance: Resistance to change is natural. Leaders need to identify the sources of resistance, address concerns empathetically, and involve resistors in the change process.

Example: *During a transition to remote work, managers might conduct surveys to understand employee concerns and provide resources and training to ease the transition.*

Adapting to Feedback: Change initiatives should be flexible and adaptive, incorporating feedback and lessons learned to improve the process and outcomes.

Example: *A company implementing agile methodologies might hold regular retrospectives to gather feedback and adjust their approach based on what is and isn't working.*

Change Management Models
Several change management models provide frameworks and tools for effectively navigating organizational change. Here are a few widely used models:

Lewin's Change Management Model: This model involves three stages: Unfreeze, Change, and Refreeze. It emphasizes preparing the organization for change, implementing the change, and solidifying the new state.

Example: *A retailer might use Lewin's model to transition from physical stores to an e-commerce platform, starting with preparing employees and customers (Unfreeze), launching the online store (Change), and integrating the new operations into the business culture (Refreeze).*

Kotter's 8-Step Change Model: Developed by John Kotter, this model outlines eight steps for successful change: Create Urgency, Form a Powerful Coalition, Create a Vision for Change, Communicate the Vision, Remove Obstacles, Create Short-Term Wins, Build on the Change, and Anchor the Changes.

Example: *A financial services firm might use Kotter's model to implement a new customer relationship management (CRM) system, following each step to ensure a smooth and effective transition.*

ADKAR Model: The ADKAR model focuses on individual change and includes five elements: Awareness, Desire, Knowledge, Ability, and Reinforcement. It emphasizes the personal journey of change and the support needed at each stage.

Example: *An educational institution might use the ADKAR model to introduce new teaching technologies, ensuring that teachers are aware of the need for change, desire to adopt the new tools, receive adequate training, and have ongoing support.*

Case Studies in Change and Transformation

Netflix's Transformation: Netflix transitioned from a DVD rental service to a leading streaming service and content creator. This transformation involved significant changes in business model, technology, and company culture.

Key Takeaway: *Embracing innovation and being willing to pivot based on market trends and consumer behavior can drive successful transformation.*

Microsoft's Cultural Shift: Under CEO Satya Nadella, Microsoft underwent a cultural transformation that emphasized collaboration, innovation, and a growth mindset. This shift supported the company's resurgence as a technology leader.

Key Takeaway: *Transformational leadership and a focus on cultural change can revitalize an organization and drive sustained success.*

General Electric's Digital Transformation: GE's efforts to become a digital industrial company involved significant investments in technology and talent, as well as changes in business processes and culture.

Key Takeaway: *Large-scale transformations require a holistic approach, addressing technology, processes, and people to achieve desired outcomes.*

Overcoming Challenges in Change Management
Navigating change comes with various challenges, including resistance, communication barriers, and maintaining momentum. Effective leaders anticipate these challenges and develop strategies to overcome them.

Addressing Resistance: Understanding the root causes of resistance and addressing them through empathy, communication, and involvement can help mitigate opposition to change.

Example: *A company facing resistance to a new performance management system might hold focus groups to understand employee concerns and adjust the system accordingly.*

Ensuring Clear Communication: Clear, consistent, and transparent communication helps manage expectations, reduce uncertainty, and build trust during change.

Example: *During a company-wide restructuring, leadership might use multiple communication channels, such as emails, meetings, and intranet updates, to keep employees informed.*

Maintaining Momentum: Sustaining momentum requires ongoing support, recognition of progress, and celebrating short-term wins to keep the team motivated and engaged.

Example: *A nonprofit organization implementing a new strategic plan might celebrate each milestone achievement, recognizing team members' contributions and maintaining enthusiasm for the initiative.*

Providing Support and Training: Ensuring that employees have the necessary skills and resources to adapt to change is crucial for successful implementation.

Example: *A hospital introducing electronic health records might offer extensive training programs and on-site support to help staff transition smoothly.*

The Role of Leadership in Change and Transformation
Leadership plays a critical role in guiding organizations through change. Effective leaders inspire confidence, foster a positive change culture, and lead by example.

Visionary Leadership: Leaders who articulate a clear and compelling vision for change can inspire and mobilize their teams towards a common goal.

Example: *A CEO launching a sustainability initiative might paint a vivid picture of the company's future as a leader in environmental stewardship, rallying employees around this vision.*

Empathetic Leadership: Demonstrating empathy and understanding the emotional impact of change on employees helps build trust and support.

Example: *A manager who acknowledges the challenges of remote work and provides flexibility and resources to support employees' well-being shows empathetic leadership.*

Transformational Leadership: Transformational leaders inspire and motivate their teams to exceed expectations, fostering innovation and a culture of continuous improvement.

Example: *A leader who encourages experimentation and rewards innovative ideas creates an environment where change is seen as an opportunity for growth.*

Resilient Leadership: Resilience is crucial for navigating the uncertainties and setbacks that often accompany change. Resilient leaders remain steadfast and adaptable, guiding their teams through challenges.

Example: *During a market downturn, a resilient leader might focus on strategic pivots and maintaining team morale, ensuring the organization emerges stronger.*

Conclusion
Navigating change and transformation is a fundamental skill for modern leaders. By understanding the dynamics of change, adopting effective change management models, and overcoming challenges, leaders can guide their organizations through successful transformations.

Leadership that combines vision, empathy, adaptability, and resilience is essential for fostering a culture that embraces change and drives continuous improvement. As organizations face an ever-evolving landscape, the ability to lead through change will remain a critical determinant of long-term success and sustainability.

CHAPTER 9: BUILDING HIGH-PERFORMANCE TEAMS

The Anatomy of High-Performance Teams
High-performance teams are distinguished by their ability to achieve outstanding results, innovate continuously, and adapt swiftly to changing conditions. Building such teams involves a deep understanding of their essential components:

Clear Goals and Roles: High-performance teams have well-defined objectives and roles. Each member understands the team's goals and their individual contributions towards achieving them.

Example: *A software development team might set a clear goal to launch a new feature by a specific date, with distinct roles such as developers, testers, and project managers clearly outlined.*

Strong Leadership: Effective leadership provides direction, support, and motivation. Leaders of high-performance teams foster trust, inspire their members, and facilitate open communication.

Example: *A project leader who regularly communicates progress, acknowledges contributions, and addresses challenges promptly can significantly enhance team performance.*

Mutual Trust and Respect: Trust and respect among team members are critical for collaboration and innovation. These teams value each member's input and foster an environment of psychological safety.

Example: In a marketing team, members freely share creative ideas without fear of judgment, knowing their contributions are respected and valued.

Effective Communication: Open and honest communication is the backbone of high-performance teams. They prioritize clear, concise, and timely communication to ensure everyone is aligned.

Example: A sales team might use regular check-ins and collaborative tools to keep everyone informed about customer feedback and sales targets.

Diverse Skill Sets: High-performance teams leverage a diverse range of skills and perspectives. Diversity enhances problem-solving and fosters innovation.

Example: A product development team might include engineers, designers, and market analysts to cover all aspects of product creation and launch.

Commitment to Continuous Improvement: These teams are committed to ongoing learning and improvement. They regularly reflect on their performance and seek ways to enhance their processes and outcomes.

Example: An agile software team conducts regular retrospectives to discuss what went well and what could be improved in their work-flow.

Building a High-Performance Team: Key Strategies

Recruitment and Selection: Hiring the right people is the foundation of building a high-performance team. Look for individuals who not only have the required skills but also fit the team culture and values.

Example: A tech start-up might prioritize candidates who demonstrate adaptability, a collaborative spirit, and a passion for innovation during the recruitment process.

On-boarding and Integration: Effective on-boarding helps new team members integrate smoothly into the team, understand their roles, and become productive quickly.

Example: A company might have a structured on-boarding program that includes mentoring, training sessions, and team-building activities.

Setting Clear Expectations: Define and communicate clear expectations regarding goals, roles, responsibilities, and performance standards.

Example: During a project kickoff meeting, a manager might outline the project scope, deadlines, and individual responsibilities to ensure everyone is on the same page.

Fostering Collaboration and Teamwork: Encourage a collaborative culture where team members support each other, share knowledge, and work together towards common goals.

Example: A finance team might use collaborative software tools to share documents and work on joint projects seamlessly.

Providing Resources and Support: Ensure that the team has the necessary resources, tools, and support to perform their tasks effectively.

Example: A creative team might be provided with the latest design software, high-quality workstations, and a conducive working environment.

Recognizing and Rewarding Performance: Acknowledge and reward team members' contributions and achievements to motivate and retain high performers.

Example: A company might have an employee recognition program that highlights outstanding contributions and provides incentives such as bonuses or professional development opportunities.

Cultivating Team Culture
A strong team culture is the backbone of high-performance teams. It encompasses shared values, behaviors, and practices that define how the team operates and interacts.

Defining Core Values: Clearly define and communicate the core values that guide the team's behavior and decision-making.

Example: *A customer service team might adopt values such as empathy, responsiveness, and excellence to guide their interactions with clients.*

Building Trust and Accountability: Foster an environment where team members trust each other and hold themselves and each other accountable for their actions and performance.

Example: *A research team might establish protocols for peer review and regular performance assessments to maintain high standards and accountability.*

Encouraging Open Communication: Promote a culture of openness where team members feel comfortable sharing ideas, feedback, and concerns.

Example: *A design team might hold regular brainstorming sessions where all members are encouraged to contribute their ideas without fear of criticism.*

Promoting Inclusivity and Diversity: Embrace diversity and inclusivity to leverage different perspectives and ideas, enhancing creativity and innovation.

Example: *A multinational corporation might implement policies that ensure diverse hiring practices and create inclusive work-spaces that respect and celebrate cultural differences.*

Facilitating Work-Life Balance: Support team members in achieving a healthy work-life balance to prevent burnout and maintain high levels of productivity and job satisfaction.

Example: *A tech company might offer flexible working hours, remote work options, and wellness programs to help employees manage their personal and professional lives effectively.*

Case Studies of High-Performance Teams

Google's Project Aristotle: Google conducted an extensive study to understand what makes high-performance teams. They found that psychological safety, dependability, structure and clarity, meaning, and impact were key factors.

Key Takeaway: Creating an environment where team members feel safe to take risks, are dependable, have clear roles, find their work meaningful, and see the impact of their efforts is crucial for building high-performance teams.

NASA's Apollo 11 Team: The team behind the Apollo 11 mission exemplifies a high-performance team. They achieved an unprecedented goal through rigorous planning, collaboration, and innovation.

Key Takeaway: Clear goals, strong leadership, meticulous planning, and a culture of collaboration and innovation can lead to extraordinary achievements.

The All Blacks Rugby Team: The New Zealand All Blacks are renowned for their high-performance culture, characterized by a strong sense of purpose, unity, and relentless pursuit of excellence.

Key Takeaway: A cohesive team culture, shared values, and a commitment to continuous improvement can drive sustained high performance in any field.

Overcoming Challenges in Building High-Performance Teams

Building high-performance teams comes with its own set of challenges. Addressing these challenges effectively is crucial for team success.

Managing Conflicts: Conflicts are inevitable in any team. Effective conflict management involves addressing issues promptly and constructively.

Example: A project manager might mediate a disagreement between team members by facilitating a discussion to understand each side's perspective and find a mutually acceptable solution.

Dealing with Under-performance: Addressing under-performance requires a combination of clear communication, support, and accountability.

Example: *A sales manager might work with an under-performing team member to identify obstacles, provide additional training, and set clear performance improvement goals.*

Maintaining Motivation: Sustaining motivation, especially during challenging times, requires regular recognition, support, and opportunities for growth.

Example: *During a tough project phase, a leader might boost team morale by celebrating small wins, offering words of encouragement, and ensuring team members feel valued.*

Balancing Individual and Team Goals: Aligning individual goals with team objectives ensures that personal ambitions contribute to the overall success of the team.

Example: *A manager might set individual performance goals that align with the team's objectives, ensuring that each member's efforts contribute to the team's success.*

Adapting to Change: Teams must be adaptable and resilient in the face of change. This involves fostering a culture that embraces change and encourages innovation.

Example: *A tech team might regularly update their skills and processes to stay ahead of industry changes and technological advancements.*

Conclusion
Building high-performance teams involves strategic recruitment, clear goals, strong leadership, and a supportive culture. By fostering trust and collaboration, leaders can create innovative and adaptable teams that consistently deliver exceptional results. The strategies in this chapter offer a guide for creating teams that drive organizational success and resilience in a dynamic business environment.

CHAPTER 10: CONFLICT RESOLUTION AND NEGOTIATION

Understanding Conflict in the Workplace

Conflict is an inevitable aspect of human interaction, particularly in the workplace where diverse personalities, goals, and perspectives converge. Understanding the nature and sources of conflict is essential for effective conflict resolution and negotiation.

Types of Conflict: Conflict in the workplace can manifest in various forms, including interpersonal conflicts between individuals, team conflicts arising from differences in goals or approaches, and organizational conflicts stemming from structural or cultural issues.

Example: An interpersonal conflict might arise between team members due to differing communication styles or personality clashes.

Causes of Conflict: Conflict can be triggered by factors such as communication breakdowns, incompatible goals or interests, scarce resources, power struggles, personality differences, or organizational changes.

Example: A conflict might arise within a team over the allocation of project resources or differing opinions on project priorities.

Impact of Conflict: Unresolved conflict can have detrimental effects on individuals, teams, and organizations, including decreased morale, productivity, and job satisfaction, increased turnover, and damaged relationships.

Example: Persistent conflict within a team might lead to absenteeism, increased stress levels, and decreased collaboration, ultimately affecting project outcomes.

Principles of Conflict Resolution

Conflict resolution is the process of addressing and resolving disputes in a constructive and mutually beneficial manner. It involves understanding the underlying causes of conflict, facilitating open communication, and seeking collaborative solutions.

Active Listening: Active listening involves fully engaging with the speaker, empathizing with their perspective, and seeking to understand their concerns without judgment or interruption.

Example: *A manager practicing active listening might paraphrase team members' concerns to ensure clarity and demonstrate understanding.*

Empathy and Perspective-Taking: Empathy involves recognizing and validating the emotions and perspectives of others, even if they differ from one's own. Perspective-taking requires stepping into the shoes of others to understand their motivations and concerns.

Example: *A team leader might acknowledge the frustrations of team members affected by a new policy change and express empathy for their challenges.*

Effective Communication: Clear and transparent communication is essential for resolving conflicts. It involves expressing oneself honestly and respectfully, actively listening to others, and seeking common ground.

Example: *A project manager might hold a team meeting to address misunderstandings and clarify expectations regarding project goals and roles.*

Collaborative Problem-Solving: Collaborative problem-solving involves working together to identify mutually acceptable solutions that address the underlying needs and interests of all parties.

Example: *A negotiation between two departments might focus on finding compromises that meet both departments' objectives while minimizing negative impacts.*

Conflict Management Styles: Different conflict management styles, such as avoidance, accommodation, competition, compromise, and collaboration, can be employed depending on the situation and the desired outcomes.

Example: *A leader might choose a collaborative approach when resolving conflicts that require creative solutions and long-term relationship building.*

Negotiation Strategies

Negotiation is the process of reaching agreements through discussion and compromise. Effective negotiation strategies can help parties achieve their goals while preserving relationships and mutual respect.

Preparation: Thorough preparation is essential for successful negotiations. This involves clarifying goals, understanding the interests and priorities of all parties, and identifying potential areas of agreement and disagreement.

Example: *Before entering salary negotiations, a job candidate might research industry standards, assess their market value, and identify their key priorities and trade-offs.*

Active Listening and Questioning: Actively listening to the other party's concerns and asking clarifying questions can help uncover underlying interests and create opportunities for collaboration.

Example: *A salesperson might listen attentively to a client's needs and ask probing questions to understand their challenges and preferences.*

Building Rapport and Trust: Building rapport and trust with the other party can create a positive negotiation environment and increase the likelihood of reaching mutually beneficial agreements.

Example: *A manager might start a negotiation meeting with informal small talk to establish rapport before delving into substantive discussions.*

Exploring Win-Win Solutions: Seeking win-win solutions that meet the interests of both parties can lead to sustainable agreements and foster long-term relationships.

Example: *In a supplier negotiation, a buyer might explore options for volume discounts or longer-term contracts that benefit both parties financially.*

Managing Emotions: Emotions can run high during negotiations, potentially derailing productive discussions. Effective negotiators remain calm, composed, and focused on the issues at hand.

Example: *A negotiator faced with aggressive tactics might acknowledge the emotions involved while steering the conversation back to the relevant facts and objectives.*

Flexibility and Creativity: Flexibility and creativity are essential for finding innovative solutions and overcoming impasses during negotiations.

Example: *In a real estate negotiation, a buyer might offer alternative terms such as a lease-to-own arrangement or seller financing to address the seller's concerns.*

Conflict Resolution Techniques

Several techniques can be employed to resolve conflicts effectively and restore positive working relationships:

Mediation: A neutral third party facilitates communication and negotiation between conflicting parties, helping them reach mutually acceptable solutions.

Example: *An HR professional might mediate a conflict between two employees by facilitating a structured dialogue and guiding them towards resolution.*

Negotiated Compromise: Parties negotiate mutually acceptable compromises that address their respective needs and interests.

Example: *In a team conflict over project deadlines, team members might negotiate a revised timeline that balances competing priorities and workloads.*

Problem-Solving Workshops: Structured workshops bring together stakeholders to collaboratively identify and address underlying issues and develop solutions.

Example: *An organization experiencing interdepartmental conflicts might organize cross-functional workshops to foster understanding and collaboration.*

Facilitated Dialogue: Facilitated dialogues provide a structured forum for parties to express their perspectives, share concerns, and explore common ground.

Example: *A community organization might facilitate a dialogue between residents and local authorities to address concerns and develop solutions to neighborhood issues.*

Case Studies in Conflict Resolution and Negotiation

Union-Management Negotiations: In labor negotiations, unions and management engage in collective bargaining to address issues such as wages, benefits, and working conditions.

Key Takeaway: Successful labor negotiations require open communication, mutual respect, and a willingness to compromise to reach agreements that benefit both parties.

International Diplomacy: Diplomatic negotiations between countries involve addressing complex geopolitical issues, often requiring skilled negotiation, diplomacy, and conflict resolution.

Key Takeaway: Diplomatic negotiations require patience, cultural sensitivity, and a focus on common interests to overcome differences and achieve peaceful resolutions.

Business Partnership Negotiations: Negotiating business partnerships involves aligning goals, interests, and expectations between companies to create mutually beneficial agreements.

Key Takeaway: Business negotiations require strategic planning, flexibility, and a focus on long-term value creation to build successful partnerships.

Overcoming Challenges in Conflict Resolution and Negotiation

Managing Power Dynamics: Power imbalances can complicate negotiations and hinder conflict resolution. Effective strategies involve acknowledging power differentials and ensuring all parties feel heard and respected.

Example: *In a negotiation between a large corporation and a small supplier, the larger party might demonstrate sensitivity to the supplier's concerns and offer concessions to address power disparities.*

Cultural Differences: Cultural differences in negotiation styles, communication norms, and conflict resolution approaches can create challenges in cross-cultural negotiations. Successful resolution involves cultural sensitivity, awareness, and adaptation to bridge cultural gaps and foster understanding.

Example: *In international business negotiations, parties might engage in cultural training, utilize interpreters, and conduct pre-negotiation research to understand cultural nuances and preferences.*

Emotional Intelligence: Emotions can cloud judgment and escalate conflicts during negotiations. Developing emotional intelligence skills, such as self-awareness, self-regulation, empathy, and social skills, can help negotiators manage emotions effectively.

Example: *A negotiator faced with a confrontational counterpart might use empathy to understand their perspective and regulate their own emotions to maintain composure and focus on productive dialogue.*

Overcoming Deadlocks: Negotiations can reach impasses where parties are unable to reach agreements. Strategies for overcoming deadlocks include exploring creative solutions, taking breaks to de-escalate tensions, and seeking assistance from mediators or facilitators.

Example: *In a business negotiation stuck on pricing issues, parties might explore alternative payment structures, introduce concessions on other terms, or bring in a neutral mediator to facilitate resolution.*

Conclusion
Conflict resolution and negotiation are essential skills for navigating the complexities of human interaction, both in the workplace and beyond. By understanding the sources of conflict, employing effective communication and negotiation strategies, and overcoming challenges, individuals and organizations can resolve disputes constructively and reach mutually beneficial agreements.

Successful conflict resolution and negotiation require patience, empathy, flexibility, and a commitment to finding win-win solutions. By cultivating these skills and approaches, individuals can build stronger relationships, enhance collaboration, and achieve better outcomes in their personal and professional lives.

As conflicts inevitably arise and negotiations become increasingly complex, the principles and techniques outlined in this chapter provide a valuable framework for resolving disputes, building consensus, and fostering productive relationships in today's interconnected and diverse world.

CHAPTER 11: FOSTERING A CULTURE OF CONTINUOUS LEARNING

The Importance of Continuous Learning
In today's rapidly evolving world, organizations and individuals must embrace continuous learning to stay competitive, adapt to change, and drive innovation. A culture of continuous learning promotes growth, development, and resilience, enabling individuals and organizations to thrive in dynamic environments.

Adapting to Change: Continuous learning equips individuals with the skills and knowledge needed to navigate evolving technologies, industries, and market trends.

Example: *A software developer who continually updates their coding skills can adapt to new programming languages and frameworks as technology evolves.*

Driving Innovation: Learning fosters creativity, critical thinking, and problem-solving abilities, driving innovation and enabling organizations to stay ahead of the curve.

Example: *A marketing team that encourages experimentation and learning from failures can generate fresh ideas and breakthrough strategies.*

Enhancing Performance: Continuous learning improves individual and organizational performance by enabling employees to develop new competencies, improve existing skills, and deliver better results.

Example: *A sales team that undergoes regular training on sales techniques and product knowledge can achieve higher sales targets and customer satisfaction ratings.*

Building a Learning Culture
Creating a culture of continuous learning requires intentional efforts to prioritize learning, provide resources and support, and foster a growth mindset throughout the organization.

Leadership Commitment: Leaders play a crucial role in setting the tone for learning and development. Leaders who prioritize and model continuous learning inspire their teams to do the same.

Example: *A CEO who regularly attends training sessions and encourages employees to pursue learning opportunities sends a clear message about the importance of continuous growth.*

Providing Learning Opportunities: Organizations should offer a variety of learning opportunities, including formal training programs, workshops, conferences, online courses, and mentoring.

Example: *A tech company might provide employees with access to online learning platforms like Coursera or Udemy, allowing them to develop technical skills at their own pace.*

Encouraging Experimentation and Risk-Taking: Creating a safe environment where employees feel encouraged to take risks, experiment with new ideas, and learn from failures fosters innovation and growth.

Example: A product development team might hold regular hackathons where employees can pitch and prototype new product ideas, regardless of whether they succeed or fail.

Recognition and Reward: Acknowledging and rewarding learning achievements reinforces the value of continuous learning and motivates employees to invest in their development.

Example: An organization might establish an employee recognition program that celebrates learning milestones, such as completing a certification or mastering a new skill.

Promoting Knowledge Sharing: Encouraging knowledge sharing and collaboration enables employees to learn from each other's experiences, expertise, and best practices.

Example: A project management team might hold regular knowledge-sharing sessions where members discuss lessons learned from past projects and share tips for success.

Overcoming Barriers to Learning

Despite the benefits of continuous learning, several barriers can hinder its adoption and implementation. Identifying and addressing these barriers is essential for fostering a culture of continuous learning.

Time Constraints: Busy schedules and competing priorities can make it challenging for employees to dedicate time to learning and development.

Example: An organization might offer flexible work hours or dedicated learning time to accommodate employees' training needs without disrupting their work-flow.

Resource Limitations: Limited access to learning resources, such as budget constraints or outdated training materials, can hinder employees' ability to engage in meaningful learning activities.

Example: *A small business might partner with educational institutions or utilize free online resources to provide cost-effective learning opportunities for employees.*

Resistance to Change: Some employees may resist learning new skills or technologies due to fear of failure, comfort with the status quo, or skepticism about the value of learning.

Example: *A manager might address resistance to change by emphasizing the benefits of learning, providing supportive coaching, and highlighting success stories of colleagues who have embraced new challenges.*

Lack of Organizational Support: A lack of support from leadership or inadequate infrastructure for learning can hinder employees' ability to engage in continuous learning.

Example: *An organization might appoint learning champions or establish a dedicated learning and development department to provide guidance, resources, and support for employees' learning journeys.*

Leveraging Technology for Learning
Technology plays a pivotal role in enabling continuous learning by providing access to a wealth of learning resources, facilitating remote learning, and personalizing learning experiences.

Online Learning Platforms: Websites, apps, and platforms such as Coursera, LinkedIn Learning, and Khan Academy offer a vast array of courses and resources on various topics, accessible anytime, anywhere.

Example: *An employee interested in improving their project management skills might enroll in an online course on project management fundamentals on a platform like Udemy.*

Virtual Training and Webinars: Virtual training sessions and webinars allow employees to participate in live or recorded training sessions, workshops, and seminars without the need for physical attendance.

Example: An organization might host a webinar series on leadership development, inviting guest speakers to share insights and best practices with employees.

Learning Management Systems (LMS): LMS platforms enable organizations to deliver, manage, and track learning activities, including course enrollment, progress tracking, and assessment.

Example: An HR department might use an LMS to administer compliance training modules, track employees' completion status, and generate reports for regulatory purposes.

Mobile Learning Apps: Mobile learning apps provide on-the-go access to learning materials, allowing employees to learn at their convenience using smart-phones or tablets.

Example: An employee commuting to work might use a language learning app like Duolingo to practice vocabulary and grammar exercises on their smart-phone.
Case Studies in Continuous Learning

Google's 20% Time: Google encourages employees to spend 20% of their time on projects outside their core responsibilities, fostering creativity, innovation, and continuous learning.

Key Takeaway: Allocating time for self-directed learning and exploration empowers employees to pursue their interests and contribute to organizational innovation.

Amazon's Career Choice Program: Amazon offers employees tuition assistance for courses in high-demand fields, enabling them to acquire new skills and advance their careers within or outside the company.

Key Takeaway: Investing in employees' education and career development not only benefits individuals but also strengthens the organization's talent pipeline and competitiveness.

Sales-force's Trailhead Platform: Salesforce's Trailhead platform provides interactive learning modules, badges, and certifications on Sales-force products and technologies, empowering users to skill up and earn credentials.

Key Takeaway: *Providing gamified learning experiences and tangible credentials motivates learners to engage in continuous learning and skill development.*

Conclusion
Fostering a culture of continuous learning is essential for organizations and individuals to thrive in today's dynamic and competitive landscape. By prioritizing learning, providing resources and support, overcoming barriers, leveraging technology, and embracing a growth mindset, organizations can create environments where learning is valued, encouraged, and celebrated.

Continuous learning not only enhances individual and organizational capabilities but also fosters innovation, adaptability, and resilience. As organizations embark on their learning journeys, the principles, strategies, and case studies outlined in this chapter serve as guiding principles for building a culture of continuous learning that drives success and sustains growth in the long term.

CHAPTER 12: LEVERAGING TECHNOLOGY AND DIGITAL TRANSFORMATION

Introduction to Digital Transformation
In the modern era, technology is at the heart of organizational success. Digital transformation refers to the integration of digital technologies into all aspects of business operations, fundamentally changing how organizations operate and deliver value to customers, employees, and stakeholders.

The Digital Landscape: The digital landscape encompasses a wide range of technologies, including cloud computing, artificial intelligence (AI), data analytics, Internet of Things (IoT), blockchain, and augmented reality (AR), among others.

Example: An e-commerce company might leverage AI-powered recommendation engines to personalize product suggestions for customers based on their browsing and purchase history.

The Need for Digital Transformation: Organizations must embrace digital transformation to stay competitive, meet evolving customer expectations, improve operational efficiency, drive innovation, and adapt to changing market dynamics.

Example: A traditional retail chain might invest in e-commerce platforms, mobile apps, and omnichannel strategies to enhance the customer shopping experience and compete with online retailers.

Key Drivers of Digital Transformation: Key drivers of digital transformation include technological advancements, changing customer behaviors and preferences, competitive pressures, regulatory requirements, and the need for operational agility and resilience.

Example: A financial institution might embark on digital transformation initiatives to enhance cybersecurity measures, comply with regulatory mandates, and streamline financial transactions.

Strategies for Digital Transformation

Successful digital transformation requires strategic planning, leadership commitment, cross-functional collaboration, and a customer-centric approach. Organizations can adopt various strategies to drive digital transformation initiatives effectively.

Vision and Leadership: A clear vision and strong leadership are essential for driving digital transformation initiatives and aligning stakeholders around common goals and priorities.

Example: *A CEO might articulate a vision for becoming a digital-first organization and appoint a chief digital officer (CDO) to lead transformation efforts and drive cultural change.*

Customer-Centric Approach: Digital transformation should focus on meeting customer needs, preferences, and expectations by delivering seamless, personalized, and value-added experiences across digital touch-points.

Example: *An airline company might invest in mobile check-in, self-service kiosks, and in-flight entertainment systems to enhance the travel experience and meet customer demands for convenience and flexibility.*

Data-Driven Insights: Leveraging data analytics and business intelligence tools enables organizations to gain actionable insights, optimize decision-making, and drive continuous improvement across all areas of the business.

Example: *An e-commerce platform might use data analytics to analyze customer behavior, predict purchasing patterns, and tailor marketing campaigns to specific customer segments.*

Agile and Iterative Approach: Adopting agile methodologies and iterative development approaches allows organizations to adapt quickly to changing requirements, prioritize initiatives based on value, and deliver incremental improvements.

Example: *A software development team might embrace agile principles such as scrum or kanban to break down projects into manageable tasks, iterate on features, and gather feedback from users.*

Partnerships and Ecosystems: Collaborating with technology partners, start-ups, and industry ecosystems enables organizations to access specialized expertise, innovative solutions, and new market opportunities.

Example: An automotive manufacturer might partner with technology companies to develop connected car solutions, autonomous driving technologies, and mobility services that enhance the driving experience and differentiate their offerings.

Implementing Digital Transformation Initiatives

Implementing digital transformation initiatives involves a structured approach, starting with assessment, planning, and prioritization, followed by execution, measurement, and continuous refinement.

Assessment and Readiness: Organizations should assess their current capabilities, identify areas for improvement, and evaluate readiness for digital transformation.

Example: A retail company might conduct a digital maturity assessment to evaluate its technological infrastructure, digital skills, customer engagement channels, and data capabilities.

Strategic Planning: Developing a digital transformation road-map involves setting strategic objectives, defining key initiatives and milestones, allocating resources, and establishing metrics for success.

Example: A health-care provider might develop a road-map for implementing electronic health records (EHR) systems, telemedicine platforms, and patient engagement solutions to improve health-care delivery and patient outcomes.

Cross-Functional Collaboration: Successful digital transformation requires collaboration across various functions, including IT, marketing, operations, finance, and human resources.

Example: A manufacturing company might establish cross-functional teams to streamline supply chain processes, optimize production work-flows, and implement Industry 4.0 technologies such as robotics and IoT sensors.

Change Management and Communication: Effective change management involves communicating the vision for digital transformation, engaging stakeholders, addressing resistance, and providing training and support.

Example: A financial services firm might conduct town hall meetings, workshops, and training sessions to educate employees about the benefits of digital transformation and address concerns about job roles and responsibilities.

Continuous Monitoring and Improvement: Monitoring progress, gathering feedback, and measuring outcomes are essential for ensuring the success and sustainability of digital transformation initiatives.

Example: A hospitality company might track key performance indicators (KPIs) such as customer satisfaction scores, website traffic, online bookings, and revenue growth to assess the impact of digital initiatives and make data-driven decisions.

Case Studies in Digital Transformation

Netflix: Netflix transformed the entertainment industry by transitioning from a DVD rental service to a digital streaming platform, leveraging data analytics, personalization algorithms, and original content production to disrupt traditional TV broadcasting models.

Key Takeaway: Embracing digital technologies and data-driven insights can revolutionize business models, enhance customer experiences, and drive market leadership.

Tesla: Tesla revolutionized the automotive industry by introducing electric vehicles with advanced autonomous driving capabilities, over-the-air software updates, and integrated renewable energy solutions.

Key Takeaway: Innovating at the intersection of hardware, software, and renewable energy technologies can create new market opportunities and redefine industry standards.

Airbnb: Airbnb disrupted the hospitality industry by creating a peer-to-peer marketplace for short-term lodging rentals, leveraging digital platforms, user-generated content, and community-driven experiences to democratize travel accommodation.

Key Takeaway: *Embracing digital platforms, ecosystems, and user-centric design principles can empower individuals, unlock untapped resources, and transform traditional industries.*

Overcoming Challenges in Digital Transformation

Digital transformation initiatives often face challenges such as legacy systems, cultural resistance, talent shortages, cybersecurity risks, and regulatory constraints. Addressing these challenges requires a holistic approach, proactive risk management, and continuous adaptation.

Legacy Systems and Technical Debt: Legacy systems and technical debt can impede digital transformation efforts by limiting agility, scalability, and interoperability.

Example: *A financial institution might prioritize modernizing core banking systems, migrating to cloud infrastructure, and adopting microservices architecture to overcome legacy constraints and accelerate innovation.*

Cultural Resistance and Change Fatigue: Cultural resistance and change fatigue can hinder adoption of new technologies and processes, leading to project delays and low morale.

Example: *An organization might invest in change management initiatives, leadership coaching, and employee engagement programs to cultivate a culture of innovation, resilience, and continuous learning.*

Talent Acquisition and Retention: Recruiting and retaining digital talent with specialized skills in areas such as data science, cybersecurity, cloud computing, and user experience design can be challenging.

Example: *A technology company might offer competitive salaries, professional development opportunities, and a supportive work environment to attract and retain top talent in a competitive market.*

Cybersecurity Risks: Digital transformation exposes organizations to cybersecurity threats such as data breaches, ransom-ware attacks, and insider threats, necessitating robust security measures and risk mitigation strategies.

Example: An organization might implement multi-factor authentication, encryption, intrusion detection systems, and security awareness training to protect sensitive data and infrastructure from cyber threats.

Regulatory Compliance and Legal Considerations: Digital transformation initiatives must comply with various regulations and legal requirements, including data privacy laws, industry standards, and intellectual property rights.

Example: A health-care provider might implement HIPAA-compliant security measures, data encryption protocols, and patient consent mechanisms to protect medical records and ensure regulatory compliance.

The Future of Digital Transformation
Looking ahead, the pace of digital transformation is expected to accelerate, driven by emerging technologies, evolving customer expectations, and global mega-trends such as urbanization, sustainability, and demographic shifts.

Emerging Technologies: Emerging technologies such as 5G, edge computing, quantum computing, biotechnology, and nanotechnology will revolutionize industries, create new business models, and transform society.

Example: Augmented reality (AR) and virtual reality (VR) technologies have the potential to revolutionize education, health-care, entertainment, and remote collaboration, offering immersive and interactive experiences.

Hyper-connected Ecosystems: Hyper-connected ecosystems will emerge, linking devices, sensors, machines, and humans in real-time networks, enabling seamless communication, automation, and decision-making.

Example: Smart cities will leverage IoT sensors, AI algorithms, and data analytics to optimize traffic flow, reduce energy consumption, enhance public safety, and improve quality of life for residents.

Digital Ethics and Governance: Digital transformation will raise ethical, social, and regulatory questions related to privacy, security, equity, accountability, and transparency, requiring careful consideration and responsible governance.

Example: *Ethical AI principles such as fairness, transparency, accountability, and privacy will guide the development and deployment of AI systems, ensuring they benefit society while minimizing unintended consequences.*

Sustainable Innovation: Sustainable innovation will drive digital transformation initiatives focused on addressing environmental challenges, reducing carbon footprint, promoting circular economy practices, and advancing social equity.

Example: *Renewable energy technologies such as solar, wind, and hydro power will play a central role in decarbonizing the energy sector, reducing greenhouse gas emissions, and mitigating climate change impacts.*

Conclusion

Digital transformation is a continuous journey that requires organizations to embrace innovation, agility, and resilience in an increasingly digital and interconnected world. By leveraging technology strategically, driving cultural change, and adopting customer-centric approaches, organizations can unlock new opportunities, create value, and achieve sustainable growth in the digital age.

As digital transformation evolves, organizations must navigate challenges, embrace emerging technologies, and uphold ethical principles to ensure responsible and inclusive innovation. By embracing digital transformation as a strategic imperative, organizations can thrive in the face of disruption, lead change, and shape the future of industries, economies, and societies.

CHAPTER 13: ETHICAL DECISION-MAKING IN A GLOBALIZED WORLD

Introduction to Ethical Decision-Making
Ethical decision-making is the process of evaluating and choosing actions that align with moral principles, values, and standards of conduct. In a globalized world characterized by diverse cultures, interconnected economies, and complex ethical dilemmas, ethical decision-making is essential for individuals and organizations to navigate moral challenges and uphold integrity.

The Importance of Ethics: Ethics guide behavior, inform decision-making, and shape relationships in personal, professional, and societal contexts. Upholding ethical principles builds trust, credibility, and reputation, fostering sustainable relationships and long-term success.

Example: *A business leader who prioritizes honesty, transparency, and fairness earns the trust and loyalty of employees, customers, and stakeholders, enhancing organizational reputation and brand value.*

Ethical Challenges in a Globalized World: Globalization presents ethical challenges such as cultural relativism, ethical dilemmas arising from cultural differences, human rights violations, environmental degradation, corruption, and economic inequality.

Example: *A multinational corporation operating in multiple countries must navigate ethical dilemmas related to labor practices, supply chain management, and environmental stewardship, balancing profit motives with social responsibilities.*

Frameworks for Ethical Decision-Making: Various ethical frameworks, such as utilitarianism, deontology, virtue ethics, and ethical relativism, provide principles and guidelines for evaluating moral dilemmas, weighing competing interests, and making ethical choices.

Example: *A health-care provider facing a resource allocation dilemma during a pandemic might use a utilitarian approach, prioritizing actions that maximize overall societal welfare and minimize harm to vulnerable populations.*

Principles of Ethical Decision-Making
Ethical decision-making is guided by core principles such as integrity, honesty, fairness, respect for others, responsibility, and accountability. These principles serve as moral compasses, guiding individuals and organizations to act ethically in challenging situations.

Integrity: Integrity involves acting consistently with ethical principles, being honest and transparent in communications, and upholding moral values even in the face of adversity or temptation.

Example: *A journalist who refuses to compromise journalistic integrity by accepting bribes or distorting facts maintains public trust and credibility, preserving the integrity of the profession.*

Honesty and Transparency: Honesty entails truthfulness, sincerity, and openness in interactions, communications, and relationships, fostering trust, credibility, and mutual respect.

Example: *A business leader who communicates openly and transparently with employees about organizational challenges, changes, and decisions builds a culture of trust and transparency, promoting employee engagement and commitment.*

Fairness and Equity: Fairness requires treating all individuals with impartiality, equality, and justice, respecting their rights, dignity, and diversity, and avoiding discrimination or favoritism based on irrelevant factors.

Example: *A hiring manager who evaluates job candidates based on merit, qualifications, and skills, rather than gender, race, or ethnicity, promotes fairness and diversity in the workplace, fostering an inclusive and equitable environment.*

Respect for Others: Respect involves recognizing and valuing the inherent worth, autonomy, and dignity of all individuals, regardless of their background, beliefs, or perspectives.

Example: *A leader who listens attentively to diverse viewpoints, encourages participation, and treats others with respect and empathy fosters a culture of inclusivity, collaboration, and mutual respect.*

Responsibility and Accountability: Responsibility entails taking ownership of one's actions, decisions, and their consequences, fulfilling obligations, and acting in the best interests of stakeholders.

Example: *A corporate executive who takes responsibility for a product recall due to safety concerns, communicates proactively with customers, and implements corrective actions demonstrates accountability and commitment to consumer safety.*

Ethical Decision-Making Process

The ethical decision-making process involves identifying ethical dilemmas, gathering relevant information, evaluating options, considering consequences, and choosing actions that align with ethical principles and values.

Identify the Ethical Dilemma: Recognize situations or decisions that present ethical dilemmas, conflicting interests, or moral ambiguity, requiring careful consideration and ethical analysis.

Example: *A software engineer discovers a security vulnerability in a product but faces pressure from management to release the product on schedule, raising concerns about potential harm to users and ethical responsibilities.*

Gather Relevant Information: Gather information, facts, and perspectives relevant to the ethical dilemma, considering diverse viewpoints, stakeholders' interests, and potential consequences of different courses of action.

Example: *The software engineer consults with colleagues, reviews industry standards, and assesses potential risks and impacts of releasing the product with the security vulnerability, weighing ethical considerations against business priorities.*

Evaluate Options and Alternatives: Evaluate potential options and alternatives for addressing the ethical dilemma, considering ethical principles, values, laws, organizational policies, and stakeholder expectations.

Example: *The software engineer considers options such as reporting the security vulnerability to management, refusing to release the product until the issue is resolved, or disclosing the vulnerability to external security experts for independent assessment.*

Consider Consequences and Trade-Offs: Consider the potential consequences, benefits, and trade-offs associated with each option, weighing short-term gains against long-term impacts on stakeholders, reputation, and organizational integrity.

Example: The software engineer assesses the potential risks of releasing the product with the security vulnerability, including potential harm to users, damage to the company's reputation, legal liabilities, and loss of trust from customers.

Make Ethical Choices and Take Action: Make ethical choices and take action based on careful ethical analysis, moral reasoning, and consideration of ethical principles, values, and responsibilities.

Example: The software engineer decides to escalate the security vulnerability to management, communicate the risks and implications transparently, and advocate for addressing the issue before releasing the product, prioritizing user safety and ethical considerations over business pressures.

Ethical Leadership and Organizational Culture
Ethical leadership sets the tone for organizational culture, shaping norms, values, and behaviors that promote ethical conduct, integrity, and accountability at all levels of the organization.

Lead by Example: Ethical leaders model ethical behavior, integrity, and transparency in their actions, decisions, and interactions, inspiring trust, respect, and commitment from employees.

Example: A CEO who demonstrates integrity, honesty, and ethical courage in challenging situations sets a positive example for employees, reinforcing organizational values and fostering a culture of integrity.

Foster Ethical Culture: Ethical leaders cultivate an organizational culture that values ethics, encourages open dialogue, and supports ethical decision-making, empowering employees to speak up, raise concerns, and uphold ethical standards.

Example: A senior executive who establishes ethics committees, conducts ethics training, and rewards ethical behavior creates an environment where employees feel empowered to act ethically and uphold organizational values.

Communicate Ethical Expectations: Ethical leaders communicate clear expectations regarding ethical conduct, policies, and standards, ensuring alignment with organizational values and legal requirements.

Example: A department manager who communicates zero-tolerance for unethical behavior, provides guidance on ethical dilemmas, and encourages employees to seek ethical advice when faced with difficult decisions sets clear expectations and reinforces ethical norms.

Promote Ethical Decision-Making: Ethical leaders provide support, resources, and guidance to employees for ethical decision-making, encouraging reflection, dialogue, and collaboration in addressing ethical dilemmas and fostering a sense of collective responsibility for upholding ethical standards.

Example: An HR director who offers ethics training workshops, provides ethical decision-making frameworks, and facilitates group discussions on real-life ethical scenarios empowers employees to navigate complex ethical dilemmas with confidence and integrity.

Hold Accountable for Ethical Breaches: Ethical leaders hold individuals and teams accountable for ethical breaches or misconduct, enforcing consequences and corrective actions while maintaining fairness, consistency, and due process.

Example: A corporate ethics committee conducts impartial investigations into allegations of ethical misconduct, applies disciplinary measures or sanctions as necessary, and communicates transparently about the outcomes, reinforcing organizational commitment to ethical integrity and accountability.

Ethical Challenges in a Globalized World
In a globalized world, ethical decision-making faces unique challenges related to cultural diversity, international business practices, geopolitical dynamics, and technological advancements. Addressing these challenges requires cross-cultural awareness, ethical sensitivity, and adaptive leadership.

Cultural Relativism: Cultural relativism poses challenges in navigating ethical dilemmas across diverse cultural contexts, where norms, values, and ethical standards may vary widely.

Example: *A multinational corporation operating in multiple countries must navigate cultural differences in business practices, labor standards, and environmental regulations, respecting local customs while upholding global ethical standards.*

Global Supply Chains: Global supply chains raise ethical concerns related to labor exploitation, human rights abuses, environmental degradation, and corporate social responsibility (CSR), requiring transparency, accountability, and responsible sourcing practices.

Example: *A fashion retailer must ensure ethical sourcing of materials, fair labor practices in manufacturing facilities, and sustainable production processes throughout the supply chain, addressing social and environmental impacts responsibly.*

Data Privacy and Security: Data privacy and security issues arise in the context of globalization, digitalization, and rapid technological advancements, raising concerns about surveillance, data breaches, identity theft, and algorithmic bias.

Example: *A technology company must prioritize data privacy and security measures, comply with data protection regulations, and mitigate risks of data misuse or unauthorized access, safeguarding user trust and privacy rights.*

Corruption and Bribery: Corruption and bribery pose ethical challenges in global business transactions, where bribery, kickbacks, and unethical practices may be prevalent in certain regions or industries, undermining fair competition, integrity, and trust.

Example: *A multinational corporation must adopt anti-corruption policies, conduct due diligence on business partners, and implement compliance programs to prevent bribery, corruption, and unethical conduct in international business dealings.*

Geopolitical Conflicts and Human Rights: Geopolitical conflicts, political instability, and human rights violations present ethical dilemmas for organizations operating in regions affected by armed conflict, repression, or human rights abuses.

Example: *A multinational corporation must assess the ethical implications of conducting business in conflict zones, respecting human rights principles, and avoiding complicity in human rights violations or atrocities.*

Conclusion
Ethical decision-making is essential for individuals and organizations to navigate the complexities of a globalized world with integrity, responsibility, and respect for ethical principles. By upholding core ethical values, fostering ethical leadership, and addressing ethical challenges proactively, individuals and organizations can build trust, credibility, and sustainability in a diverse and interconnected global environment.

As ethical dilemmas continue to evolve in the face of globalization, technological advancements, and geopolitical dynamics, ethical decision-making remains a cornerstone of ethical leadership and organizational integrity. By embracing ethical principles, promoting ethical culture, and making ethical choices guided by moral values and responsibilities, individuals and organizations can contribute to a more just, equitable, and sustainable world.

CHAPTER 14: THE FUTURE OF LEADERSHIP

Introduction to Future Leadership
The landscape of leadership is continuously evolving in response to technological advancements, demographic shifts, socio-economic changes, and global challenges. As we look to the future, new paradigms of leadership are emerging, characterized by agility, adaptability, inclusivity, and ethical stewardship.

Dynamic Leadership Context: The future of leadership is shaped by dynamic forces such as digitalization, globalization, automation, climate change, and geopolitical shifts, requiring leaders to navigate complexity, uncertainty, and rapid change.

Example: *A technology leader must anticipate disruptive trends, embrace innovation, and lead digital transformation initiatives to stay competitive in a fast-paced, tech-driven market.*

Emerging Leadership Models: New models of leadership emphasize collaboration, empowerment, and distributed decision-making, moving away from hierarchical command-and-control structures towards more agile, networked, and inclusive approaches.

Example: *A startup founder adopts a servant leadership approach, empowering team members, fostering creativity, and cultivating a culture of autonomy and accountability to drive innovation and growth.*

Global Leadership Competencies: Global leaders must possess a diverse skill set encompassing cultural intelligence, cross-cultural communication, global mindset, and ethical leadership, enabling them to lead effectively in multicultural environments and navigate complex geopolitical dynamics.

Example: *An international NGO leader demonstrates cultural sensitivity, empathy, and diplomacy in engaging with diverse stakeholders, building partnerships, and advancing global development goals.*

Characteristics of Future Leaders
Future leaders embody a range of characteristics and competencies that enable them to thrive in an increasingly complex and interconnected world.

Adaptive Agility: Future leaders are adaptable and agile, capable of embracing change, learning from failure, and pivoting quickly in response to shifting circumstances and emerging opportunities.

Example: *An entrepreneur demonstrates resilience and flexibility in adapting business strategies, seizing market opportunities, and iterating on product innovation to stay ahead of competitors in a rapidly changing industry.*

Inclusive Leadership: Future leaders embrace diversity, equity, and inclusion, creating environments where all individuals feel valued, respected, and empowered to contribute their unique perspectives and talents.

Example: *A corporate executive promotes diversity and inclusion initiatives, advocates for equitable hiring practices, and fosters a culture of belonging and psychological safety, driving innovation and employee engagement.*

Digital Fluency: Future leaders possess digital fluency and technological acumen, leveraging digital tools, data analytics, AI, and automation to drive organizational transformation, optimize processes, and deliver value to stakeholders.

Example: A digital strategist harnesses data analytics and AI algorithms to analyze customer insights, personalize marketing campaigns, and optimize digital experiences, driving customer engagement and loyalty.

Purpose-Driven Leadership: Future leaders are guided by a sense of purpose and social responsibility, aligning organizational goals with broader societal needs, environmental sustainability, and ethical stewardship.

Example: A social entrepreneur launches a mission-driven start-up focused on addressing environmental challenges, promoting renewable energy solutions, and fostering sustainable development, creating positive impact beyond financial returns.

Collaborative Influence: Future leaders excel at collaborative leadership, building cross-functional teams, fostering synergy, and mobilizing collective efforts towards shared goals and outcomes.

Example: A community organizer brings together diverse stakeholders, including government agencies, NGOs, businesses, and residents, to address social issues, advocate for policy change, and drive community development initiatives.

Future Leadership Trends and Challenges
Several trends and challenges are shaping the future of leadership, influencing leadership styles, organizational dynamics, and strategic priorities.

Remote Work and Virtual Leadership: The rise of remote work and virtual teams presents opportunities and challenges for leaders in managing distributed teams, fostering collaboration, and maintaining organizational culture and cohesion.

Example: A remote team leader leverages digital collaboration tools, virtual team-building activities, and clear communication channels to support remote employees, enhance productivity, and maintain team morale.

Digital Transformation and Innovation Leadership: Digital transformation and innovation leadership are critical for organizations to stay competitive, adapt to technological disruptions, and capitalize on emerging opportunities in the digital economy.

Example: A chief innovation officer leads digital transformation initiatives, fosters a culture of experimentation and learning, and champions disruptive technologies such as AI, blockchain, and IoT to drive innovation and growth.

Ethical Leadership and Responsible Governance: Ethical leadership and responsible governance are imperative for addressing ethical dilemmas, upholding integrity, and building trust in the face of growing scrutiny from stakeholders, regulators, and the public.

Example: A corporate board chairperson oversees governance practices, ensures ethical compliance, and holds management accountable for ethical conduct, promoting transparency and accountability in corporate decision-making.

Crisis Leadership and Resilience: Crisis leadership and resilience are essential for navigating unexpected disruptions, such as pandemics, natural disasters, geopolitical crises, and economic downturns, while maintaining business continuity and safeguarding organizational stability.

Example: A crisis response team leader coordinates emergency preparedness efforts, crisis communications, and risk mitigation strategies, mobilizing resources and stakeholders to respond effectively to crises and minimize impacts.

Sustainable Leadership and Environmental Stewardship: Sustainable leadership and environmental stewardship are critical for addressing pressing environmental challenges, such as climate change, resource depletion, and biodiversity loss, and promoting sustainable business practices.

Example: A sustainability officer develops and implements sustainability strategies, sets environmental targets, and engages stakeholders in sustainability initiatives, driving progress towards carbon neutrality, circular economy, and social responsibility goals.

Conclusion
The future of leadership is dynamic, diverse, and driven by a rapidly changing global landscape. As organizations navigate complex challenges and seize new opportunities, future leaders must embody adaptive agility, inclusive leadership, digital fluency, purpose-driven values, and collaborative influence to drive innovation, resilience, and sustainable growth.

By embracing emerging leadership models, cultivating leadership competencies, and addressing future leadership trends and challenges, individuals and organizations can navigate uncertainty, inspire positive change, and shape a brighter future for themselves, their organizations, and society as a whole.

CHAPTER 15: BUILDING RESILIENT ORGANIZATIONS

Introduction to Organizational Resilience
Organizational resilience is the ability of a company to anticipate, adapt to, and recover from disruptions, challenges, and crises while maintaining core functions and strategic objectives. In an increasingly volatile and uncertain world, building resilient organizations is essential for ensuring sustainability, competitiveness, and long-term success.

Understanding Resilience: Resilience goes beyond mere survival; it encompasses proactive risk management, strategic foresight, and adaptive capacity to thrive in the face of adversity.

Example: A resilient organization not only weathers economic downturns but also leverages them as opportunities for innovation, growth, and transformation.

Components of Organizational Resilience: Organizational resilience comprises various components, including robust risk management, agile decision-making, effective crisis response, flexible operations, and strong leadership.

Example: *A multinational corporation develops contingency plans, invests in supply chain diversification, and fosters a culture of adaptability to mitigate risks and enhance resilience against geopolitical disruptions.*

The Business Case for Resilience: Building resilient organizations yields tangible benefits, such as enhanced competitiveness, operational efficiency, brand reputation, stakeholder trust, and long-term value creation.

Example: *A resilient company that anticipates market trends, invests in innovation, and fosters employee well-being outperforms competitors, attracts investors, and retains customers even during turbulent times.*

Strategies for Building Organizational Resilience

Building organizational resilience requires a proactive and holistic approach that integrates risk management, strategic planning, operational excellence, and cultural transformation.

Risk Identification and Assessment: Organizations must identify and assess potential risks, vulnerabilities, and disruptions across internal and external environments, considering various scenarios and their potential impacts.

Example: *A financial institution conducts risk assessments to identify cybersecurity threats, regulatory changes, economic fluctuations, and other external risks that could affect its operations and stakeholders.*

Strategic Planning and Scenario Analysis: Strategic planning involves scenario analysis, contingency planning, and risk mitigation strategies to anticipate and prepare for various future scenarios, ensuring flexibility and agility in response to changing conditions.

Example: *An energy company develops scenario plans for different climate change scenarios, such as extreme weather events, regulatory changes, and shifts in consumer preferences, to inform strategic investments in renewable energy and sustainability initiatives.*

Operational Resilience and Business Continuity: Operational resilience entails robust infrastructure, redundant systems, and backup plans to maintain critical functions and services during disruptions, minimizing downtime and financial losses.

Example: *An e-commerce retailer implements redundant servers, cloud-based backups, and disaster recovery protocols to ensure website uptime, secure customer data, and fulfill orders even during cyber-attacks or system failures.*

Supply Chain Resilience and Diversification: Supply chain resilience involves diversifying suppliers, mapping dependencies, and building redundancy to mitigate risks of disruptions, such as natural disasters, geopolitical tensions, or supply chain disruptions.

Example: *An automotive manufacturer diversifies its supply chain, sources components from multiple regions, and maintains strategic inventories to reduce reliance on single suppliers and minimize risks of production delays.*

Crisis Management and Communication: Effective crisis management requires clear communication, decisive leadership, and coordinated response efforts to address emergencies, mitigate impacts, and restore normal operations.

Example: *A hospitality company activates its crisis management team, communicates with guests and employees transparently, and implements safety protocols and contingency plans during a natural disaster or public health crisis.*

Learning and Adaptation: Resilient organizations foster a culture of continuous learning, innovation, and adaptation, encouraging experimentation, feedback, and reflection to improve processes, products, and practices.

Example: A technology company conducts post-mortem analyses of project failures, encourages knowledge sharing, and incentivizes employees to propose innovative solutions, fostering a culture of resilience and continuous improvement.

Building a Resilient Organizational Culture
Organizational resilience is not just about structures and processes; it is also about cultivating a resilient culture that values adaptability, collaboration, accountability, and learning.

Leadership Commitment: Resilient organizations start with leadership commitment to resilience as a strategic priority, setting the tone from the top and championing resilience initiatives across the organization.

Example: *A CEO demonstrates commitment to resilience by allocating resources, empowering resilience teams, and integrating resilience considerations into strategic decision-making and governance processes.*

Employee Engagement and Empowerment: Engaged and empowered employees are essential for building organizational resilience, as they contribute diverse perspectives, creativity, and problem-solving skills to resilience efforts.

Example: *A manufacturing company involves front-line workers in identifying operational risks, implementing safety protocols, and suggesting process improvements, empowering employees as active participants in building resilience.*

Cross-Functional Collaboration: Resilient organizations break down silos and foster cross-functional collaboration, enabling teams to work together seamlessly to address complex challenges and capitalize on opportunities.

Example: *A pharmaceutical company establishes cross-functional crisis response teams comprising representatives from R&D, manufacturing, supply chain, and regulatory affairs to coordinate pandemic response efforts and accelerate vaccine development.*

Adaptive Learning and Innovation: Resilient cultures promote adaptive learning and innovation, encouraging experimentation, knowledge sharing, and continuous improvement to stay ahead of the curve and adapt to changing circumstances.

Example: *A financial services firm implements agile methodologies, design thinking workshops, and hackathons to foster a culture of innovation, agility, and resilience in response to evolving customer needs and market trends.*

Ethical Leadership and Trust: Ethical leadership builds trust and credibility, enhancing organizational resilience by fostering transparency, integrity, and accountability in decision-making and stakeholder relationships.

Example: *An organizational leader demonstrates ethical leadership by prioritizing employee well-being, upholding ethical standards, and communicating transparently with stakeholders during challenging times, earning trust and loyalty from employees, customers, and investors.*

Conclusion
Building resilient organizations requires a proactive and integrated approach that encompasses risk management, strategic planning, operational excellence, and cultural transformation. By investing in resilience initiatives, fostering a resilient culture, and embracing adaptive strategies, organizations can navigate uncertainty, capitalize on opportunities, and thrive in an increasingly complex and interconnected world.

As organizations face evolving challenges and disruptions, resilience becomes not only a strategic imperative but also a competitive advantage, enabling organizations to withstand shocks, bounce back from setbacks, and emerge stronger and more agile than before. By building resilience into their DNA, organizations can create lasting value, inspire confidence, and shape a more sustainable and resilient future for themselves and their stakeholders.

CHAPTER 16: LEADING WITH PURPOSE AND VISION

Introduction to Purposeful Leadership
Leading with purpose and vision involves aligning organizational goals and actions with a compelling purpose and a clear vision of the future. Purposeful leaders inspire and motivate others by articulating a shared sense of purpose, defining a compelling vision, and guiding strategic initiatives that drive meaningful impact and value creation.

The Power of Purpose: Purpose is the driving force behind organizational success, motivating employees, engaging stakeholders, and guiding decision-making towards meaningful outcomes.

Example: *A social enterprise dedicated to environmental sustainability harnesses the collective purpose of employees, partners, and customers to drive positive change and create a more sustainable future.*

The Role of Vision: Vision provides a road-map for the future, guiding strategic direction, setting ambitious goals, and inspiring action towards a common aspiration or desired outcome.

Example: *A technology company's vision of creating a world where everyone is connected drives innovation, investment in infrastructure, and product development efforts to bridge the digital divide and empower communities globally.*

Purpose-Driven Leadership: Purpose-driven leaders embody authenticity, integrity, and a genuine commitment to serving a higher purpose beyond profit, inspiring trust, loyalty, and engagement from stakeholders.

Example: *A nonprofit leader dedicated to social justice leads with purpose, advocating for equity, fairness, and empowerment, mobilizing communities and driving systemic change towards a more just and inclusive society.*

Elements of Purposeful Leadership
Purposeful leadership encompasses several key elements that enable leaders to articulate a compelling purpose, define a visionary future, and mobilize others towards shared goals and aspirations.

Clarity of Purpose: Purposeful leaders articulate a clear and compelling purpose that defines the organization's reason for existence, its values, and its impact on society.

Example: A health-care leader's commitment to improving patient outcomes and enhancing public health serves as a unifying purpose that inspires health-care professionals, caregivers, and stakeholders to deliver exceptional care and innovation.

Strategic Vision: Purposeful leaders develop a strategic vision that outlines ambitious goals, long-term objectives, and a road-map for achieving the organization's mission and fulfilling its purpose.

Example: A visionary entrepreneur's bold vision of transforming transportation through sustainable mobility solutions inspires investment in electric vehicles, renewable energy infrastructure, and smart mobility technologies to reduce carbon emissions and combat climate change.

Authentic Leadership: Purposeful leaders lead with authenticity, integrity, and a genuine commitment to their organization's purpose and values, earning trust and respect from followers.

Example: A corporate executive's transparent communication, ethical decision-making, and genuine concern for employee well-being create a culture of trust, accountability, and purpose-driven performance, fostering employee engagement and organizational success.

Inspirational Communication: Purposeful leaders communicate their vision and purpose with passion, conviction, and clarity, inspiring others to share their enthusiasm and commitment to achieving shared goals.

Example: A political leader's compelling speeches, storytelling, and advocacy for social justice galvanize public support, mobilize grassroots movements, and drive policy change towards a more equitable and inclusive society.

Empowering Leadership: Purposeful leaders empower others to contribute their talents, ideas, and perspectives towards achieving the organization's purpose and vision, fostering a culture of collaboration, innovation, and shared ownership.

Example: A team leader empowers employees to take ownership of projects, make decisions autonomously, and contribute creatively to achieving team goals, fostering a sense of ownership, accountability, and pride in collective accomplishments.

Leading Change with Purpose and Vision

Purposeful leaders drive change initiatives with purpose and vision, guiding organizational transformation, innovation, and growth towards a better future.

Change Leadership: Purposeful leaders lead change initiatives with empathy, resilience, and a focus on driving positive outcomes that align with the organization's purpose and vision.

Example: A change agent leads a cultural transformation initiative, championing diversity, inclusion, and belonging as core values that drive organizational performance, innovation, and employee engagement.

Innovation Leadership: Purposeful leaders foster a culture of innovation, experimentation, and learning, encouraging creativity, risk-taking, and adaptability to drive continuous improvement and breakthrough innovation.

Example: An innovation leader empowers cross-functional teams to explore new ideas, test hypotheses, and prototype solutions, fostering a culture of curiosity, collaboration, and agility that fuels innovation and drives competitive advantage.

Transformational Leadership: Purposeful leaders drive organizational transformation by aligning strategic initiatives, allocating resources, and empowering teams to adapt, evolve, and thrive in a rapidly changing environment.

Example: A transformational leader leads a digital transformation initiative, leveraging emerging technologies, agile methodologies, and change management best practices to modernize processes, enhance customer experiences, and drive business growth.

Sustainable Leadership: Purposeful leaders embrace sustainable leadership practices, integrating environmental, social, and governance (ESG) considerations into strategic decision-making and business operations.

Example: *A sustainable leader implements sustainability initiatives, such as renewable energy investments, waste reduction programs, and community engagement projects, aligning business objectives with environmental stewardship, social responsibility, and long-term value creation.*

Conclusion

Leading with purpose and vision is essential for driving organizational success, inspiring innovation, and fostering resilience in an ever-changing world. Purposeful leaders articulate a clear sense of purpose, define a compelling vision, and mobilize others towards shared goals and aspirations, creating a sense of meaning, belonging, and fulfillment.

As organizations face evolving challenges and opportunities, purposeful leadership becomes a strategic imperative for driving transformation, innovation, and sustainable growth. By embodying authenticity, integrity, and a genuine commitment to serving a higher purpose, purposeful leaders can inspire positive change, build trust, and shape a better future for themselves, their organizations, and society as a whole.

CHAPTER 17: THE ROLE OF MENTORSHIP AND COACHING IN LEADERSHIP DEVELOPMENT

Introduction to Mentorship and Coaching
Mentorship and coaching play vital roles in leadership development, providing guidance, support, and feedback to aspiring and experienced leaders alike. By leveraging the wisdom, experience, and insights of mentors and coaches, leaders can accelerate their growth, expand their skills, and unlock their full potential.

The Importance of Mentorship and Coaching: Mentorship and coaching are essential components of leadership development, offering personalized guidance, constructive feedback, and tailored support to individuals at various stages of their leadership journey.

Example: A seasoned executive mentor provides career advice, shares industry insights, and offers leadership coaching to a high-potential employee, helping them navigate career challenges and develop leadership skills.

Key Differences Between Mentorship and Coaching: While mentorship involves a long-term, nurturing relationship focused on personal and professional growth, coaching is a more structured, goal-oriented process aimed at enhancing specific skills or addressing performance gaps.

Example: A mentor provides career guidance, role modeling, and advice based on personal experience, while a coach uses questioning, active listening, and skill-building exercises to help a leader develop specific competencies or overcome challenges.

Benefits of Mentorship and Coaching: Mentorship and coaching offer numerous benefits, including accelerated learning, increased self-awareness, improved decision-making, enhanced performance, and career advancement.

Example: A mentee gains valuable insights, perspectives, and career opportunities through their mentor's guidance, while a coaching client develops new skills, strategies, and self-confidence to overcome obstacles and achieve goals.

The Role of Mentors in Leadership Development

Mentors play a critical role in leadership development by providing guidance, support, and wisdom based on their own experiences and expertise.

Guidance and Advice: Mentors offer valuable guidance and advice on career development, leadership challenges, and professional growth opportunities, drawing on their own successes and failures.

Example: *A mentor advises a new manager on effective leadership strategies, communication techniques, and conflict resolution skills, helping them navigate their new role with confidence and competence.*

Networking and Relationship Building: Mentors facilitate networking and relationship-building opportunities, connecting mentees with influential contacts, mentors, and peers who can support their career advancement.

Example: *A mentor introduces a mentee to industry leaders, professional associations, and networking events, expanding their professional network and opening doors to new career opportunities.*

Role Modeling and Inspiration: Mentors serve as role models and sources of inspiration, demonstrating leadership qualities, values, and behaviors that inspire and motivate mentees to strive for excellence.

Example: *A mentor exemplifies integrity, resilience, and empathy in their leadership style, inspiring their mentee to emulate these qualities and develop their own authentic leadership style.*

The Role of Coaches in Leadership Development

Coaches play a crucial role in leadership development by providing objective feedback, challenging assumptions, and facilitating growth through structured coaching processes.

Objective Feedback and Assessment: Coaches provide objective feedback and assessment on leadership strengths, weaknesses, and blind spots, helping leaders gain self-awareness and identify areas for improvement.

Example: *A coach conducts a 360-degree feedback assessment, gathers input from colleagues, direct reports, and supervisors, and provides insights and recommendations to help the leader enhance their leadership effectiveness.*

Skill Development and Performance Improvement: Coaches facilitate skill development and performance improvement through targeted coaching interventions, skill-building exercises, and action-oriented development plans.

Example: *A coach helps a leader develop effective communication skills, conflict resolution techniques, and emotional intelligence competencies through role-playing, feedback sessions, and real-world application.*

Accountability and Goal Setting: Coaches hold leaders accountable for their goals and commitments, providing structure, support, and accountability to ensure progress and sustained growth.

Example: *A coach helps a leader set SMART goals, define action steps, and establish accountability mechanisms to track progress, celebrate achievements, and overcome obstacles on their leadership development journey.*

Integrating Mentorship and Coaching in Leadership Development Programs

Effective leadership development programs integrate mentorship and coaching components to provide a comprehensive and personalized approach to leadership development.

Structured Mentorship Programs: Organizations establish structured mentorship programs that pair mentees with experienced mentors based on mutual interests, goals, and developmental needs.

Example: *A corporate mentorship program matches high-potential leaders with senior executives or seasoned professionals who serve as mentors, providing ongoing support, guidance, and career advice.*

Professional Coaching Services: Organizations offer professional coaching services to leaders at all levels, providing access to certified coaches who specialize in leadership development, executive coaching, and career transition coaching.

Example: *A leadership development initiative includes one-on-one coaching sessions, group coaching workshops, and online coaching resources to support leaders in developing specific leadership competencies and achieving their career goals.*

Peer Coaching and Mentoring Circles: Organizations facilitate peer coaching and mentoring circles where leaders can exchange insights, share experiences, and support each other's growth and development.

Example: *A peer mentoring circle brings together leaders from diverse backgrounds and industries to share best practices, seek advice, and provide peer support in navigating leadership challenges and opportunities.*

Conclusion
Mentorship and coaching are indispensable components of effective leadership development, providing personalized guidance, support, and feedback to aspiring and experienced leaders alike. By leveraging the wisdom, experience, and insights of mentors and coaches, leaders can accelerate their growth, expand their skills, and unlock their full potential, ultimately driving organizational success and creating a positive impact in their communities and beyond.

www.ingramcontent.com/pod-product-compliance
Lightning Source LLC
Chambersburg PA
CBHW070344230526
45471CB00006B/2428